Cambridge Elements ≡

Elements in Religion and Monotheism
edited by
Paul K. Moser
Loyola University Chicago
Chad Meister
*Affiliate Scholar, Ansari Institute for Global Engagement with Religion,
University of Notre Dame*

MONOTHEISM AND PLURALISM

Rachel S. Mikva
Chicago Theological Seminary

CAMBRIDGE
UNIVERSITY PRESS

Shaftesbury Road, Cambridge CB2 8EA, United Kingdom

One Liberty Plaza, 20th Floor, New York, NY 10006, USA

477 Williamstown Road, Port Melbourne, VIC 3207, Australia

314–321, 3rd Floor, Plot 3, Splendor Forum, Jasola District Centre, New Delhi – 110025, India

103 Penang Road, #05–06/07, Visioncrest Commercial, Singapore 238467

Cambridge University Press is part of Cambridge University Press & Assessment, a department of the University of Cambridge.

We share the University's mission to contribute to society through the pursuit of education, learning and research at the highest international levels of excellence.

www.cambridge.org
Information on this title: www.cambridge.org/9781009500463

DOI: 10.1017/9781009273374

First published 2024

A catalogue record for this publication is available from the British Library.

ISBN 978-1-009-50046-3 Hardback
ISBN 978-1-009-27338-1 Paperback
ISSN 2631-3014 (online)
ISSN 2631-3006 (print)

Cambridge University Press & Assessment has no responsibility for the persistence or accuracy of URLs for external or third-party internet websites referred to in this publication and does not guarantee that any content on such websites is, or will remain, accurate or appropriate.

Monotheism and Pluralism

Elements in Religion and Monotheism

DOI: 10.1017/9781009273374
First published online: March 2024

Rachel S. Mikva
Chicago Theological Seminary
Author for correspondence: Rachel S. Mikva, rmikva@ctschicago.edu

Abstract: Can monotheistic traditions affirm the comparable value of diverse religions? Can they celebrate our world's multiple spiritual paths? This Element explores historical foundations and contemporary paradigms for pluralism in Judaism, Christianity, and Islam. Recognizing that there are other ways to interpret the traditions, it excavates the space for theological parity.

This Element also has a video abstract: Cambridge.org/ERM_Mikva

Keywords: pluralism, theology, Christianity, Islam, Judaism

ISBNs: 9781009500463 (HB), 9781009273381 (PB), 9781009273374 (OC)
ISSNs: 2631-3014 (online), 2631-3006 (print)

Contents

1 Pluralism and Monotheism

1.1 What Is Pluralism?

The Pluralism Project at Harvard University defines pluralism as actively seeking understanding across lines of difference. Diversity is the simple fact of people with different religious, racial, ethnic, gender, and other identities living or working near one another; pluralism requires "energetic engagement." Aiming to make room for conflicting truth claims and avoid the artificial construction of others, the Pluralism Project's definition additionally emphasizes an encounter of commitments based on dialogue.[1] Religious pluralism is related to but distinct from tolerance, which suggests forbearance in response to ideas and practices believed to be inferior or incorrect – extended as a favor rather than for our mutual benefit. Many scholars have designated specific qualities that facilitate a pluralist ethos, including hospitality, humility, empathy, conscience, and a capacity for ambiguity. It entails efforts to humanize and maintain respect for the irreducible otherness of those we encounter.[2]

Theologies of religion, however, often deploy the term "pluralism" in a different sense: It represents the conviction that religious value exists in a diversity of traditions, potentially equally valid and sufficient on their own. This usage traces back at least to Alan Race's 1982 book *Christians and Religious Pluralism*, in which he offered three approaches to the multiplicity of spiritual lifestances[3]: exclusivism, inclusivism, and pluralism.

In the basic template, an exclusivist maintains that one's own religious tradition represents the only way to truth, salvation, redemption, or the divine. Pluralists affirm the sufficiency and efficacy of other lifestances and the value of multiple spiritual paths in the world. Inclusivist attitudes stand somewhere in the middle, encompassing a variety of theologies and perspectives that see beauty in multiple religious paths but claim one religion is superior and perhaps necessary to all others. A classic inclusivist position was articulated by theologian Karl Rahner, who spoke of "anonymous Christians" – people of diverse faiths who were recipients of God's grace due to the salvific work of Jesus Christ.[4]

Race's analysis has been critiqued on multiple counts: for its construction around Christian questions of salvation, which are not pertinent to every lifestance; for ignoring intrafaith diversity; for identifying too few or too

---

[1] The Pluralism Project, "About" (Harvard University, 2008), https://pluralism.org/about. See also Eck, *A New Religious America*, 70–71.

[2] See, for example, Cornille, *Im-Possibility of Interreligious Dialogue*; Landau, "Interfaith Leadership Training at Hartford Seminary;" Patel, *Interfaith Leadership*.

[3] Harry Stopes-Roe introduced the term life stance (here "lifestance") to provide inclusive language for secular, humanist, and religious orientations. See "Humanism as a Life Stance," 19–21.

[4] Imhof and Biallowons (eds.), *Karl Rahner in Dialogue*, p. 207.

many approaches; and more. There are also a number of religious traditions that delineate a particular path not intended to be universal, so they do not require a theology of religions that explains the multiplicity of lifestances. It is as natural as the diversity of flora and fauna on the earth. While the criticisms are valid, this Element treats Race's categories as a valuable foundation, and they remain influential: "[I]t seemed to bring clarity to decades, if not centuries, of ecclesial and intellectual assessments of religious difference, and quickly became the prevailing intellectual framework for understanding this issue, rehearsed in countless academic treatments."[5]

The invitation from Cambridge University Press to contribute a volume on *Monotheism and Pluralism* for the Elements Series on Monotheism, edited by Chad Meister and Paul Moser, clearly had such a framework in mind.

It is helpful to think about "pluralisms" in the plural, however. One does not need to embrace the parity of multiple traditions to be a pluralist, according to the Pluralism Project definition, which establishes a broader space for efforts to advance interreligious understanding. Consequently, I distinguish the *theological* project by utilizing the term "theological pluralism." Or, to integrate nontheistic perspectives, I more often employ the phrase "parity pluralism" – careful to clarify that it refers to comparable value, not sameness.[6]

The variety of pluralist approaches within and among lifestances also argues for thinking in the plural. There are convergent or nonconvergent theories, sometimes described as identist versus differential.[7] Convergent frameworks see the multiplicity of spiritual lifestances as different experiences and interpretations of the same transcendent reality. (Perennial philosophy takes a similar approach.) Nonconvergent theologies emphasize an irreducible difference and maintain that even conflicting notions of truth, salvation, revelation, or the divine may be of comparable value. Within these categories, there are diverse arguments rooted in diverse traditions.

1.2 Why Monotheism?

Why focus here on monotheistic orientations? Many people presume that monotheism is naturally more exclusivist than other lifestances. One God – Creator of the universe, involved in history – has implications for all of creation. Consider, for example, David Hume's remarks in the ninth section of his seminal *work Natural History of Religion* (1757):

---

[5] McCarthy, *Interfaith Encounters in America*, p. 24.

[6] Mikva, *Interreligious Studies*, pp. 31, 67–91.

[7] See Olawoyin, "Varieties of Religious Pluralism," 50–58; McCarthy, *Interfaith Encounters*, pp. 27–28.

While one sole object of devotion is acknowledged, the worship of other deities is regarded as absurd and impious. Nay, this unity of object seems naturally to require the unity of faith and ceremonies, and furnishes designing men with a pretence for representing their adversaries as profane, and the objects of divine as well as human vengeance. For as each sect is positive that its own faith and worship are entirely acceptable to the deity, and as no one can conceive that the same being should be pleased with different and opposite rites and principles, the several sects fall naturally into animosity, and mutually discharge on each other that sacred zeal and rancour, the most furious and implacable of all human passions.[8]

We can dispute the notion that monotheistic traditions are uniquely problematic in this regard. Most lifestances have articulated in some form that theirs is the best, and "sacred zeal" does not appear to require a singular God. Religious and secular worldviews of all sorts have inspired animosity and violence as they sought to assert their power and impose their truth over populations throughout history.

In fact, one could deploy Race's tripartite paradigm to analyze political, philosophical, and ethical systems. Some present their own worldviews as uniquely true and necessary for human fulfillment (exclusivism), or as the analytical lens through which all other systems of thought and practice can be understood (inclusivism), or as one of multiple fruitful ways to organize the polity and understand the human (pluralism). We also know that philosophical or theological hospitality can exist alongside cultural, racial, and other types of hostility.

Yet there are specific challenges to monotheistic traditions in exploring the possibilities of pluralism. Affirming one God of all the world raises questions about the relationship of the divine to other peoples and lifestances; does God favor those who are of the faith, or guide and care for all peoples equally? In what ways is God available to them? Some traditions ask: Can they get to heaven or be saved? Such questions represent one aspect of the sustained tension between universality and particularity, but there are others. How should people of different religions be treated? Is the teaching meant for all the world? If so, why does there continue to be a multiplicity of spiritual lifestances?

Questions of truth – disclosed rather than discovered – constitute another pressing concern. With revelation and/or incarnation as historical sources of authority, conflicting ideas about the divine or what is required of human beings can be seen as challenges to the very foundations of the religion. Proscriptions of idolatry and polemic against religious others are embedded in sacred texts; if these teachings have abiding relevance, how can one affirm parity? Some

---

[8] Hume, *Dialogues and Natural History of Religion*, p. 162.

pluralist analyses make room for other monotheistic religions but struggle to recognize the validity of humanist or polytheistic perspectives because it is difficult to affirm theistic, atheistic, cosmic, and acosmic convictions as equally true.

The stakes in this work are high. As the planet becomes increasingly global and interconnected, the diversity of spiritual lifestances is more visible. Migration patterns have made it more tangible and widespread. Proximity, however, does not guarantee harmony; in fact, increased diversity left unengaged threatens social cohesion. Religious conflicts, large and small, continue to plague our society – including violence and oppression rationalized by religious claims. There is a surge in anti-Muslim bigotry, antisemitism, and xenophobia. Although religion is rarely the singular or even central cause of conflict – more often catalyzed by social, economic, and political claims – it continues to be a fault line along which people divide.[9] Religious values, beliefs, and narratives give ultimate purpose to the struggle, frequently framed by a moral binary of good and evil.

Yet, sustained encounters between people who orient themselves around religion differently have also mobilized individuals and communities to work together for the common good in a vast array of interfaith efforts. It has inspired people to reexamine their assumptions about different lifestances and the teachings that underlie them. Scholars and religious leaders have discovered within their traditions multiple paths toward theological pluralism.

This study concentrates on such analyses. While there is ample text and history that justify exclusivist or inclusivist perspectives, they are not the only possibilities. Section 4 addresses challenges to parity pluralism and some of the responses, but this volume is not designed to debate the superiority of one perspective. It is excavating space for theological pluralism without denying that there are other ways to read the traditions. Navigating religious difference in our spiritually diverse world is tremendously important and theology plays a role, making an exploration of pluralism within monotheism a valuable tool for coexistence.

There are numerous monotheistic traditions, including Bahá'í, Druze, Rastafari, Mormon, Samaritan, Sikh, Zoroastrian, and Vaishnava Hindu perspectives. Although this Element concentrates on the three religions that readers shaped by Western culture more frequently call to mind, namely Judaism, Christianity, and Islam, the choice reflects the limits of my expertise rather than a preference. Word limits also circumscribe the discussion, allowing only for an overview of pluralist voices. There is much more that could be said.

---

[9] Sacks, *The Dignity of Difference*, pp. 5–6.

The focus on Judaism, Christianity, and Islam also highlights coformative dimensions of religious identity and theology, given the communities' substantive interaction and mutual influence over the centuries. While self and other are always mutually constituted, Jews, Christians, and Muslims have often been the most proximate others – geographically, historically, and religiously – and they have depicted each other as a means to define themselves. "While difference or "otherness" may be perceived as being either LIKE-US or NOT-LIKE-US, it becomes most problematic when it is TOO-MUCH-LIKE-US or when it claims to BE-US. It is here that the real urgency of theories of the 'other' emerges, called forth not so much by a requirement to place difference, but rather by an effort to situate ourselves."[10]

1.3 About the Author

Since there is no view from nowhere, I should situate myself. I am a creature of the Western, secularized academy. My location in the United States, reading primarily English-language scholarship, shapes my worldview as well as the voices I include. Additionally, when I engage in the study of scriptures, I understand them all as human documents. Although I sometimes employ conventional language that suggests a certain event or quote rendered in the text is historically accurate (e.g., Jesus said, God instructed), it is presented "as if," recognizing the profound ways in which the authors strive to capture and convey their experience of the divine. At the same time, I refuse to hold historical criticism as the litmus test for responsible exegesis, since the religious traditions developed their own rigorously critical tools. Premodern interpretation has much to teach about how to read scripture.

While this Element provides a review of other scholars' theologies rather than my own, I am also a parity pluralist. I believe that religions are diverse languages by which we come to experience transcendent aspects of our universe, to explore our essential purpose, and to express teachings that can help us embody it. Our brains are wired to learn religion as they are wired to absorb language. They are all translations of something ineffable, and no one can claim primacy. In fact, the polyphonic chorus is part of the beauty of human experience. My pluralist commitment includes an equal embrace of secular humanism and other lifestances that do not fit the classic understanding of religion but nonetheless have language to articulate transcendence, purpose, and an ethical path for living. It also seeks to include nonpluralist perspectives in some fashion so that pluralism does not accidentally create

---

[10] Smith, *Relating Religion*, p. 245.

a new hierarchy of religions. I view this work as Gustavo Gutierrez describes liberation theology, as a "hermeneutic of hope."[11]

1.4 About the Element

Monotheism and Pluralism provides an introduction to various pluralist theologies in Judaism, Christianity, and Islam. Section 2 explores historical foundations in sacred texts and premodern teachings. Although the current age especially presses for an embrace of diversity, awareness of religious difference is not new, and the traditions offer a rich array of perspectives.

Many of the contemporary pluralist theologies described in Section 3 are rooted in these precedents. While each tradition has unique questions and its own history of interpretation, there is also significant overlap in pluralist strategies. Some are epistemological, recognizing the limits of human understanding in ways that constrain religious absolutism. Some are sociological, reckoning with the reality of countless intelligent, ethical people of other faiths and none. Some raise theological challenges to exclusivism: How could a God who is both loving and powerful be so uncaring or so incompetent that only a small portion of humanity has it right after all these years? And many pluralist voices raise questions about ethics, grappling with the role of religion in justifying harm to our neighbors on scales large and small. As S. Mark Heim wrote, "Before it is any kind of theory, pluralism is a commitment to exorcise the religious sources of human oppression."[12]

Section 4 investigates various critiques of theological pluralism, including:

- Scholars distort traditions to yield values that align with modernity.
- They promote intellectually unsustainable conclusions and/or a debilitating relativism.
- Pluralism tends to universalize Western values and establish itself as the most highly evolved position.

Some critiques relate to broader concerns about theologies of religion, which often limit what gets counted as religion, privilege Christian and theistic concerns, or develop *a priori* metatheories that do not reckon with particularity and complexity in religious difference. The section also incorporates pluralists' rejoinders to these critiques.

The final section of the Element offers a preliminary investigation of religious pluralism in its broader understanding. There are scholars and others who,

---

[11] Gutierrez, "Hermeneutic of Hope," 9.

[12] Heim, *Salvations*, p. 72. For a delineation of pluralist strategies, see Griffin, "Religious Pluralism," in Griffin, *Deep Religious Pluralism*, pp. 3–38.

either because of their religious commitments or their analysis of pluralist logics, cannot affirm parity pluralism – but still seek a way to be accountable to the ethical demands of religious diversity.

2 Historical Perspectives

Monotheistic traditions are not monolithic in their approach to religious difference. This section explores scriptural and historical voices that contribute to pluralist thought, revealing internal multiplicity and dynamism. It includes mainstream concepts that serve as foundations for contemporary theology, as well as proto-pluralist possibilities that challenged historical orthodoxy. Although the themes overlap within Jewish, Christian, and Islamic teachings, here each tradition is treated separately.[13]

Most of the pertinent texts specifically address the existence of religious others or the ways in which followers are instructed to think about revelation and scripture. Traditional sources demonstrate an awareness of multivocality in sacred texts and their exegesis, as well as the provisional nature of truth and the human role in discerning the Word. Valuing the role of doubt as a part of faith, they call for epistemological humility. They also express consciousness of historical change and its impact on religious meaning. These teachings do not constitute theological pluralism in the modern sense, but they are self-critical tools that guard against absolutist forms of the traditions. Collectively, they nurture the roots of pluralist interpretations.

2.1 Judaism

The Hebrew Bible (Tanakh) is an anthology of books that represent diverse theologies and historical contexts. The redaction itself intimates that monotheism is a fluid, polymorphous concept:

> The dominant picture is of the god Yahweh as the supreme and primary God, at least of Israel. Yet equally obviously, the Bible preserves many traces, and in some cases more than a trace, even a little discussion, of other deities. The biblical authors, it appears, were constantly reconsidering the matter of who Yahweh is and in what his power consists.[14]

Tanakh's theological dynamism is reflected in multiple experiences of the Divine. The festivals' agricultural origins are transformed into historical events that emphasize God's involvement with the nation's destiny, while the prophets radiate God's passion for justice, and wisdom literature is consumed by

---

[13] Parts of this section are adapted from Rachel S. Mikva, *Dangerous Religious Ideas*; the arguments are detailed there at greater length.

[14] Machinist, "Once More," 37.

theological perplexities.[15] Sometimes a shift is explicit: In Exodus 6:2, for example, God is portrayed instructing Moses to share a divine name that is different from the one the patriarchs knew – YHWH rather than El-Shaddai. In small but significant ways, the sacred text makes room for change in religious thought so that no word is absolute.

The text also grapples with the limits of our understanding. Moses' experience in Exodus 33–34, where he begs to see God's glory, hints at apophatic theology. God's response is to reveal relational qualities, including lovingkindness and forgiveness of transgression, but not the divine essence: "You cannot see My face for no one shall see My face and live" (Exod 33:20). Recognition that our perceptions of God are partial and provisional, an insight repeated throughout history in all three traditions, is an essential foundation for numerous pluralist theologies.

Multiple passages speak of God's relationship with other nations. The eighth-century BCE prophet Amos taught that God's special connection to Israel in no way precludes redemptive work with others. "YHWH proclaims: Are you not like the Kushites to me, O people of Israel? Did I not bring Israel out of the land of Egypt, and the Philistines from Caphtor, and the Arameans from Kir?" (Amos 9:7). His contemporary Micah proclaimed an ideal vision of the future in which all peoples will walk in the names of their gods, even as the people of Israel forever walk in the name of YHWH (Mic 4:5). These perspectives indicate, at the very least, that a universal God does not require a universal religion.

Respect for the fact that others worship differently is expressed in the Septuagint rendering of Exodus 22:27 as well: "Do not revile *elohim*." Although the Hebrew term *elohim* is multivalent and the verse likely commands the people not to revile judges, it can also refer to god(s) – which is how the Greek translation renders it (*theous*). Josephus, a first-century Greek-speaking Jewish historian, remarked, "Our legislator has expressly forbidden us to blaspheme the gods recognized by others, out of respect for the very name God" (*Contra Apionem* 2.237). His slightly older contemporary Philo, an Alexandrian philosopher and commentator, read the verse similarly and cautioned that religious antagonism inevitably leads to war (*Questions and Answers on Exodus* 2.5).

Whispers of proto-pluralist thought in later Jewish tradition repeatedly cite verses from Tanakh to support their insights. The psalmist sang that YHWH is close to all who call upon God in truth (145:18), and the twelfth–thirteenth-century Provençal exegete David Kimchi commented that it does not matter

---

[15] Shachter, *The Idea of Monotheism*, pp. 2–4.

what people (read: religion) they are from as long as their mouth and heart align.[16] Jeremiah 23:29 asserts that God's word is like fire, like a hammer striking rock – an image that conjures an effusion of sparks and signifies multiple possibilities of meaning. Rabbi Yishmael (second century) interpreted the verse to mean that every word spoken by the Holy One divided into seventy languages, suggesting a polyphony that goes beyond Jewish understanding alone (*b. Shabbat* 88b).

There is a poetic and powerful passage in the Tosefta, a collection of rabbinic teachings redacted in the second century. In response to a question about how to (literally, *why*) learn Torah when one sage permits and another prohibits the same action, it examines the various verses of God revealing divine "words" and asserts, "All the words have been given by a single Shepherd: One God created them, one Provider gave them, the Lord of all deeds, blessed be He, has spoken them. So make yourself a heart of many rooms" (*t. Sotah* 7:12). The heart in rabbinic imagination is the seat of the mind, and "a heart of many rooms" is likely a helpful image for how to retain knowledge that does not have a single, direct answer; it does not necessarily argue for the modern pluralism we might hear in such a phrase. Furthermore, we must acknowledge that the passage's affirmation of diverse voices is limited, representing only the community of sages and those who followed them. Yet it clearly claims that all their opinions derive from God, giving divine authorization to multivocality.

Rabbinic culture embraced multiple schools of thought and canonized controversy, increasingly raising up internal pluralism as an ideological value in subsequent generations. Unpacking the brief disagreements found in the Mishnah and Tosefta with elaborate analysis, discussions in the Talmud tend to maintain the validity of conflicting viewpoints – grounding each one deeply in the soil of scripture – rather than resolve the argument. Local variation is affirmed by statements such as, "Each river follows its own course" (*b. Hullin* 57a; *b. Gittin* 60b).

Certain passages have become the poster children of Talmudic pluralism, including a repeated trope that identifies all the contradictory opinions from the sages as the word of the living God (*b. Eruvin* 13b; *b. Gittin* 6b; *y. Yevamot* 1:6 (3b)). Another suggests that the argument is what substantiates Torah in the life of the community: "Had the words of Torah been given as clear-cut decisions, it would not have a leg to stand on" (*y. Sanhedrin* 4:2 (22a)). Even God is portrayed as involved in rabbinic controversy, studying the opinions of the

---

[16] Radak, "Radak on Psalms145:18," *Sefaria*, www.sefaria.org/Radak_on_Psalms.145.18? lang=bi. See also Jospe, "Pluralism out of the Sources of Judaism: The Quest for Religious Pluralism without Relativism," in Goshen-Gottstein and Korn, *Jewish Theology and World Religions*, p. 120.

sages, disagreeing with the heavenly academy, and occasionally deferring to the earthly one (*b. Bava Metzi'a* 86a). Disagreement and difference play a uniquely important role in fulfilling the Word.

Moshe Halbertal, a modern orthodox scholar, has asked the crucial question, "How does the canonization of controversies relate to the problem of truth in interpretation, especially when the word of God is concerned?"[17] One way of thinking about this issue is to consider what the rabbis meant when they asserted that divergent ideas are all the word of the living God. Did they mean that God intended multiple senses, either simultaneously or for different circumstances? Or were the rabbis being authorized to distill God's purposes, by which legitimate processes of interpretation could yield equally legitimate alternatives? Or is divine meaning singular, with the rabbis striving toward the single correct answer based on proper procedure? Not surprisingly, each of these possibilities can be found within Jewish tradition.

One rabbinic saying that recognizes how revelation is adapted for particular contexts is *dibra Torah kileshon benei adam* ("Torah speaks in the language of human beings"). When sages of the classical period first invoked this principle, they meant that one should not overread the text. Yet the great medieval Spanish philosopher and commentator Abraham ibn Ezra (1089–1167) understood it as a hermeneutical principle of accommodation. He assumed that divine revelation was adapted to the capacity of ancient Israel to receive it, affirming the human role in interpretation and opening the doorway to change. God's teaching is continually adjusted to "the process of intellectual, moral, and even political advancement of [humanity]."[18]

Rabbinic appreciation for the paradox of the eternal and eternally changing notion of Torah is perhaps best encapsulated in a Talmudic aggadah that imagines Moses sitting in Rabbi Akiba's classroom in the second century CE. He is completely lost and sits in the back (the sign of a beginner). When one of the students asks Rabbi Akiba for the source of his knowledge, however, Akiba replies, "It is from Moses on Sinai," and Moses is comforted (*b. Menaḥot* 29b). Whether meant as metaphorical transmission or historical fact, the passage reckons with how tradition is remolded in each generation. The result may be unrecognizable to its forebears, but it stands as an authentic embodiment of Torah teaching. With the meanings of scripture always in flux, we should not imagine that our understanding reflects God's ultimate purposes.

Additionally, the value of human reason is well-established in the tradition, even though the rabbis recognized that it would sometimes be in tension with revelation. There are at least fourteen instances in the Babylonian Talmud in

---

[17] Halbertal, *People of the Book*, p. 46.   [18] Funkenstein, *Perceptions of Jewish History*, p. 88.

which a rabbinic dispute was explained by determining that one sage relied on scriptural interpretation in his decision, and one relied on reason – both legitimate ways of trying to discern truth. There are also over two hundred instances in which the rabbis suggested that the biblical text "should" be different than it is.[19] Although they generally found ways to reconcile the text with what they thought was correct, they repeatedly affirmed the exercise of their God-given intellect, free will, and moral capacity.

The sages knew that proper procedure would not always yield the best answer, even if it was technically correct. In such cases, they privileged overarching values that the law was meant to embody – justice, equity, compassion, humility, righteousness, and peace, for example – naming this functional emphasis as *lifnim m'shurat hadin*, literally "within the measure of the law" but generally understood as transcending the letter of the law. The phrase affirms resolutions that are not *against* the law but focus on higher principles – at the same time that it admits the human element in interpretation.[20]

Ultimately, rabbinic explication of scripture is not about the pursuit of "truth." Describing halakhah, the rabbinic praxis developed to flesh out the values of Torah, Yale scholar Christine Hayes explains, "Rabbinic literature reflects a desire to discern what is just, equitable, pious and obedient to God's will in the realm of human behavior and to do so through interpretation and debate, rather than ratiocination from first principles." Philosophy aims to describe "a uniform and eternal truth," while rabbinic Judaism addresses "the shifting conditions of human existence."[21] Such an approach embeds an ultimate contingency in the authority of Written and Oral Torah, without succumbing to relativism and postmodern indeterminacy.[22]

Like the biblical dialectic, rabbinic teachings both affirmed human agency and acknowledged the limits of human understanding, with the latter being a common theme during the Middle Ages. Ferreting out a difficulty in Genesis 2, the influential thinker Moses Maimonides (1138–1204) wondered why God would not want human beings to eat from the tree of knowledge of good and evil. Would it not be of benefit, providing the necessary understanding to make moral choices? His interpretation of the narrative held that we had a superior knowledge before eating from this tree – knowledge of truth and falsity. All we have after violating the divine command is relative judgment, uncertainly

---

[19] Kraemer, *Mind of the Talmud*, p. 146.
[20] See Berman, "*Lifnim Mishurat Hadin*;" Hayes, *What's Divine about Divine Law?*, pp. 171–245.
[21] Hayes, "Legal Truth, Right Answers and Best Answers," 86.
[22] Kolbrener, "Chiseled on All Sides," 277. For extended discussion regarding truth in Jewish tradition, see Goshen-Gottstein (ed.), *Religious Truth*.

grounded in personal feelings about right and wrong, contingent upon culture and context (*Guide for the Perplexed* I:2).

Maimonides particularly stressed epistemological humility in relation to our understanding of God's essence, claiming that we can make no true affirmative statement about the nature of the divine. The best we can do is to speak in negative terms – for example, "God is not lacking in power." In other words, God has power but does not possess it in a way that is comparable to anything else (*Guide* I:56–59). Along with this "negative theology," he also established an intellectual distinction between faith and certainty. He argued, for instance, that traditional and metaphysical reflection led him to affirm the creation of the universe in time, but neither creation ex nihilo nor the eternality of the universe could be demonstrably proven. His conviction was a matter of faith, not certainty (*Guide* II:25).[23]

Rabbinic literature discusses various questions related to religious "others." For example, the prominent rabbinic leader Saadia Gaon (c. 882–942) warned the Jewish community not to misconstrue the idea of Israel as God's special possession; all nations belong to God, and Israel's election does not imply exclusion of others.[24] As the prophet Amos had cautioned long before, chosenness entails accountability to the covenant of Torah rather than favorable treatment (Amos 3:2).

One question that is frequently raised in interfaith conversations today focuses on whether access to *olam haba*, a Hebrew term for the afterlife (literally, "the next world"), is seen as reserved for Jews or not. Long ago, Rabbi Joshua b. Hananiah (first to second century) argued that the righteous of all nations are included (*t. Sanhedrin* 13.2; *b. Sanhedrin 105a),* and his opinion quickly became normative.[25]

Righteousness among the nations was sometimes measured based on the rabbinic concept of Noahide laws. Interpreting Genesis 9:9, in which God makes a covenant with all of humanity after the flood, the sages imagined a kind of natural law that includes seven elements: a requirement to establish laws and to prohibit blasphemy, adultery, bloodshed, theft, consuming the blood of a living animal, and idolatry (*b. Sanhedrin* 56a). The list thus prompts questions of whether a particular religion is idolatrous or not.

---

[23] See Pines, "The Limitations of Human Knowledge," 82–109.

[24] Saadia Gaon, *Book of Beliefs and Opinions*, pp. 18, 104, 125–126 (Introduction and Article 2). In his introduction, Saadia attempted to delineate the requirements of monotheism, recognizing that it is not simply a matter of religious identity. See also Bachya ibn Pakuda, *Duties of the Heart*, I: 1–2.

[25] See also Maimonides, *Mishneh Torah*, Laws of Repentance 3:5. For discussion of non-Jews in rabbinic literature, see Porton, *Goyim*; Hayes, "The 'Other' in Rabbinic Literature," 243–269.

The Catalan medieval scholar Menachem Meiri (1249–c. 1315) argued that Christianity and Islam are not idolatrous because they have moral codes and a way of life in service to God. With a close reading of Exodus 20:3, he emphasized that it is a command *to Israel* not to have other gods; as long as they embrace a moral code, other peoples may have other gods. Meiri taught that all people who sincerely profess an ethical religion are part of a greater spiritual Israel.[26]

Maimonides asserted that Muslims and Christians play a significant role in God's redemptive plan, preparing "the whole world to worship God with one accord."[27] The Danish scholar Jacob Emden (1697–1776) similarly claimed that "the Nazarene" did much good by leading Gentiles to embrace Torah and move away from idolatry. He opined that assemblies of Christians and Muslims are also "for the sake of Heaven" and that God grants prophecy to the worthy among them.[28] Although these perspectives still suggest that monotheism should be universal, there is also the rabbinic concept of *shituf*, a notion that other lifestances may perceive partners/co-participants with the one God.[29] It foreshadows contemporary convictions of convergent pluralism that imagine all religions are directed toward the same transcendent reality, even as they understand it differently (see Section 3).

One of the most remarkable medieval Jewish voices is that of twelfth-century Yemenite mystic Natan'el al-Fayyumi. He taught that God sent prophets to all the nations, each suited to their time and place, to guide manifold peoples to righteousness. He specifically affirmed Muhammad as a prophet for Muslims, emphasizing that everyone should fulfill what was revealed to them.[30] Influenced by the Ismaili Brethren of Purity, his writings echo some of the more pluralist *ayat* in the Qur'an. Al-Fayyumi's embrace of multiple revelations goes beyond most of his contemporaries, even though medieval Jewish scholars accepted the idea that wisdom and truth could be found outside of Judaism.

---

[26] See his Talmud commentary, *Beit haBekhira*, on *b. Bava Qamma* 37b; 113a-b; *b. Bava Metzi'a* 59a; *Avodah Zarah* 26a; *Horayot* 11a for a range of his rulings and reasoning; see also Halbertal, "Ones Possessed of Religion." In the Talmud, Rabbi Yohanan argued that everyone who repudiated idolatry could be called *Yehudi* – a Jew (*b. Megillah* 13a).

[27] In the same text, however, he lamented the enormous harm wrought by Christianity, causing "Jews to be slain by the sword, their remnants to be scattered and dishonored, the Torah to be altered, and the majority of the world to err and serve a god other than YHWH." Maimonides, *Mishneh Torah, Melachim* 11: 4.

[28] Emden, in a responsum republished as an appendix to his commentary on *Seder Olam Rabbah veZuta*, and in *Lechem Shamayim*. See Falk, "Rabbi Jacob Emden's Views on Christianity," 105–111.

[29] See Alon Goshen-Gottstein, "Encountering Hinduism: Thinking Through *Avodah Zarah*," in Goshen-Gottstein and Korn, *Jewish Theology and World Religions*, pp. 263–298.

[30] Al-Fayyumi, *Bustan al-Ukul*, pp. 104–109.

At the cusp of modernity, such robust pluralist arguments became more common. A compelling example is this open letter that Moses Mendelssohn (1729–86, Germany) wrote to Swiss clergyman Johann Kaspar Lavater, rejecting pressure to convert to Christianity. Although it is clearly an argument for Jewish particularity, it expresses a broadly pluralist perspective based on ethical criteria:

> If a Confucius or a Solon were to live among our contemporaries, I could, according to my religion, love and admire the great man without succumbing to the ridiculous desire to convert him. Convert a Confucius or a Solon? What for? ... And as far as the general principles of religion are concerned, we should have little trouble agreeing on them. Do I think he can be saved? It seems to me that anyone who leads men to virtue in this life cannot be damned in the next.[31]

Mendelssohn also recognized that religions may be "best" for their followers without asserting absolute supremacy: "I grant that we believe that our religion is the best because we believe it to be divinely inspired. Nevertheless, it does not follow from this premise that it is absolutely the best. It is the best religion for ourselves and our descendants, the best for certain times, circumstances and conditions."[32]

Rabbi Israel Lipschitz (1782–1860), a traditionalist from Danzig, recognized that there are many pious and ethical non-Jews, leading him to offer a substantively pluralist understanding in his Mishnah commentary: Every people has its own divine religion, which comprises three foundational principles – belief in a revealed teaching, belief in reward and punishment, and belief in an afterlife.[33] As acknowledged in Section 1, there are certainly inclusivist and exclusivist perspectives within the long history of Jewish thought, but it is not hard to find foundations on which to build a pluralist Jewish theology.

2.2 Christianity

The New Testament stands as Christianity's foundational witness to multivocality. Like the Tanakh, its collection of books speaks with various voices, but it is more explicitly a synchronic portrait of diversity in the emerging Church. The eponymous books ascribed to Matthew, Mark, Luke, and John all present themselves as "the gospel according to. . .," and they contain significant differences that attest to the subjective ways in which individuals understand

---

[31] Mendelssohn, "Letter to Johann Casper Lavater," 269.

[32] Mendelssohn, *Jerusalem and Other Jewish Writings*, p. 134.

[33] Lipschitz, *Tiferet Yisrael, Avot 3:17*, cited in Alan Brill, *Judaism and Other Religions*, p. 114.

religious experience. The ratification of four canonical gospels "introduces a principle of mutual correction and limitation whereby each Gospel is deprived of pre-eminence or complete validity" – challenging notions of inerrancy and ultimacy.[34]

The Epistles frequently grapple with growing differences in practice among the community as the teachings spread (e.g., Rom 14–15; 1 Cor 11). Their mix of Pauline and non-Pauline perspectives "form an effective, self-correcting interplay of theological and ethical concepts" – legitimizing ecclesial variety and modeling how biblical diversity enhances the life of the Church.[35]

In the early centuries, many disputes were left unresolved; those that addressed essential theological questions were debated and decided by majority vote in various councils called over the centuries. Faith in the dual nature of Jesus as both fully human and fully divine, for example, was not determined until the Council of Chalcedon in 451 CE. And still, minority opinions about such issues did not disappear.

Even the term "heresy" was not always seen in a negative light. Origen (184–253 CE) embraced its original Greek denotation, "choice" or perhaps "faction," to defend Christianity against a philosophical critique that viewed lack of agreement as a sign of falsehood. He maintained that "heresies of different kinds have never originated from any matter in which the principle involved was not important and beneficial to human life." They were necessary in the development of Christian teaching, he argued – emerging not from schism and strife but from the earnest desire of intelligent individuals, "led by certain plausible reasons to discordant views" (*Contra Celsum* 3.12–13). Ironically, Origen was later accused of heresy for some of his heterodox ideas, but he was still enormously influential and is considered by many to be a "Father of the Church."

As Christian orthodoxy became established, it was accompanied by an anachronistic mythology that godless error – represented by anything that diverges from established dogma or praxis – entered Christianity after the apostles died. Tertullian, for instance, maintained that truth always precedes counterfeit, and the Church is charged with reestablishing the former. It erased the internal pluralism of early Christianity that, in fact, came first and was deeply embedded in the development of Christian scripture, exegesis, theology, and institutions.[36]

---

[34] Gamble, *The New Testament Canon*, p. 76.

[35] Wall, "Ecumenicity and Ecclesiology," 184–185.

[36] Eusebius, *Ecclesiastical History* 3.32.7–8; Tertullian, *De praescriptione haereticorum,* p. 29. See also Bauer, *Orthodoxy and Heresy in Earliest Christianity.*

At times, however, multivocality was still celebrated. Writing about the command to "increase and multiply" (Gen 1:28), Augustine (354–430 CE) offered a meditation on exegesis that acknowledged its subjective nature. He believed open-ended reading strategies to be intended by God:

> Consider the verse "In the Beginning, God made heaven and earth." Scripture presents this truth to us in one way only, and there is only one way in which the words can be shaped by the tongue. But it may be understood in several different ways without falsification or error because various interpretations, all of which are true in themselves, may be put upon it. The offspring of men increase and multiply in this way. (*Confessions* 13.24)

William of Auvergne (c. 1180–1249) described all of scripture as a divine textbook for varying levels of students, with deliberate multiplicity. He used a range of metaphors: a mine with distinct veins of precious metals, a garden of delights, a wine cellar, a medicine chest, and a table set with a rich assortment of different dishes where each guest finds food that appeals most.[37] A divine commitment to speak to the human heart, adapting as necessary to time, place, and individual character, makes room for ongoing change.

Anselm of Havelberg (1100–58) focused on change over time, insisting that "this variety is explained not on account of the mutability of an immutable God who is 'always the same and whose years shall have no end' (Ps 101:28), but on account of human infirmity, which is mutable and on account of temporal changes from age to age" (*Dialogues* I.13, 117). *Scriptura humane loquitur*, medieval exegetes taught, mirroring the Jewish maxim that Torah speaks in the language of human beings. This principle of accommodation was sometimes deployed to justify Christian supersessionism, identifying the "old law" of Judaism as a temporary measure to prepare for the coming of Christ (e.g., Aquinas, *Summa Theologiae* I-II.98).

Yet these complex, dynamic conceptions of faith and scripture all mitigate against the ultimacy of the text and the abuse of biblical authority. It is not simply the idea that the understanding of God's teachings evolves, but a consciousness that religious truths are not eternal, that all we might consider absolute is only provisional. Origen implied that the new covenant was itself a temporary accommodation: Jesus' incarnation served as a revelation of the Divine to guide the faithful from flesh to spirit, but it is only a "shadow" until humanity grows ready for a full realization of heavenly truth (*On First Principles* II.6.7).

We also find, as in Judaism, a strong current of epistemological humility when it comes to God and God's purposes. Early thinkers like Clement of

---

[37] Benin, *Footprints of God*, p. 181.

Alexandria (c. 150–215), Basil the Great (330–379), Gregory of Nyssa (c. 335–395), John Chrysostom (347–407), and John of Damascus (c. 675–749) declared that no human term or concept could capture the reality of God. According to Cyril of Jerusalem (fourth century), "We explain not what God is but candidly confess that we have not exact knowledge concerning Him. For in what concerns God, to confess our ignorance is the best knowledge" (*Catechetical Homilies* 6.2).[38] The most influential early expressions of this idea came from Pseudo-Dionysius (sixth century), who felt that even describing God through negation was too presumptuous; his apophatic theology was popular among Christian mystics. "Cause of all existence, and therefore itself transcending existence, it alone could give an authoritative account of what it really is."[39]

Medieval Christian thinkers like Thomas Aquinas (1225–74) and St. John of the Cross (1542–91) built on this strain of apophatic theology. Nicholas of Cusa (1401–64) borrowed the term "learned ignorance" from Augustine; recognizing the limitations of human understanding made it possible to accept multiple rites and schools of Christian thought.[40] In an edited volume on learned ignorance in the Abrahamic traditions, James Heft describes the resulting space for doubt as an instrument of pluralism:

> An emphasis on learned ignorance, or the realization among learned people that their grasp of reality is inescapably limited, prevents all forms of fundamentalism, which assumes that believers are in perfect possession of ultimate reality. Once that illusion is fixed in believers' minds, all that remains is to force their belief on others. But Judaism, Christianity, and Islam all affirm that God alone is absolute and that all affirmations about God and God's revelation are inescapably limited.[41]

Addressing how we might come to know truth given such limitations, Augustine argued that everything is known merely as God makes it manifest to us (*De magistro* 12.40; *Confessions* 12:25). Aquinas' *Summa Theologiae* sought to approach truth through dialectical argument, explicitly drawing out diverse perspectives. Other medieval Christian scholars like Anselm of Canterbury (c. 1033–1109) spoke of a thing being true when it conformed to divine intent for its creation – a teleological theory of truth with results similar to the rabbis' "within the measure of the law" and to later readers who reinterpreted passages to privilege what they understood to be God's

---

[38] Acts 17:23 speaks of the "unknown God," perhaps the earliest Christian apophatic statement.
[39] Pseudo-Dionysius, *Pseudo-Dionysius*, 49–50.   [40] Casarella (ed.), *Cusanus*.
[41] Heft, "Learned Ignorance," in Heft, Firestone, and Safi, *Learned Ignorance*, p. 4.

overarching purposes.[42] Abolitionists who invoked God's commitment to liberation and love of neighbor in order to argue against scriptural sanction of slavery, for example, saw biblical truth in this way.

Absolute truth was qualified in new ways as we moved toward modernity. Søren Kierkegaard (1813–55) defined truth as "objective uncertainty, held fast in an appropriation process of the most passionate inwardness," and declared it "the highest truth available for an existing person." He also emphasized truth as that which is most relevant to our existence. Even if it were possible to establish the historical veracity and authentic inspiration of scripture without "a single little dialectical doubt," he cautioned, it would bring one no closer to faith – a posture that can only be approached subjectively.[43]

Christian attitudes about people of other lifestances shifted at different times and in different places, with pluralist-leaning attitudes being most common where Christians did not hold power. When they were being persecuted by pagan authorities, for example, Lactantius (240–320) wrote a passionate brief for freedom of religious conscience, challenging the pagan authorities' claim that they sought to promote Christian welfare by calling them to a good mind: "Do they then strive to effect this by conversation, or by giving some reason? By no means; rather, they endeavor to effect it by force and tortures. O wonderful and blind infatuation! It is thought that there is a bad mind in those who endeavor to preserve their faith, but a good one in executioners."

He proclaimed that "nothing is so much a matter of free-will as religion." Without it, religion ceases to exist (*Divine Institutes 5:19*).

An eighth-century stele engraved by Nestorian Christians in China, where Christians were a minority, celebrated an imperial proclamation with a proto-pluralist theology: "Right principles have no invariable name, holy men have no invariable station; instruction is established in accordance with the locality, with the object of benefiting the people at large."[44] The Nestorian bishop Timothy I (eighth to ninth century) affirmed that Muhammad "walked in the path of the prophets."[45] In India, the Thomas Christians affirmed "that everyone may be saved in his own law, all which are good and lead men to heaven." Although this view was condemned as heretical by the sixteenth-century Portuguese Synod at Diamper, it seemed perfectly natural for Christians in India to imagine that followers of Hindu traditions could be saved through their own *dharma*.[46]

---

[42] See Anselm of Canterbury, *De veritate* 2 and his preface; also Aquinas, *De veritate* Q1.A1–3; Suchocki, "To Tell the Truth," in Helmer and De Troyer, *Truth*, 219–223.

[43] Kierkegaard, *Concluding Unscientific Postscript*, I: 203.

[44] Schmidt-Leukel, *Religious Pluralism and Interreligious Theology*, chap. 2.

[45] Siddiqui, *Christians, Muslims, and Jesus*, p. 48.

[46] Synod of Diamper (1599), Act III, Decree 4. See K. P. Aleaz, "Pluralism Calls for Pluralistic Inclusivism: An Indian Christian Experience," in Knitter, *Myth of Religious Superiority*, p. 163.

After the fall of Constantinople in 1453, Nicholas of Cusa recounted a vision that portrayed religious violence and coercion as contrary to God's will:

> The King of heaven and earth stated that the sad news of the groans of the oppressed had been brought to him from this world's realm: because of religion many take up arms against each other and by their power either force men to renounce their long-practiced tradition or inflict death on them. There were many bearers of these lamentations from all the earth.[47]

Some proto-pluralist precedents emerged amidst Christian strongholds. Aquinas studied Greek philosophy, for example, using the work of Ibn Rushd (Avicenna), a Muslim philosopher, and Moses Maimonides, a Jewish one, to guide him. Although Aquinas was clearly not a pluralist, it is worth noting:

> What many regard as the classical Christian synthesis of philosophical theology, Aquinas' *Summa Theologiae*, proves in retrospect to have already been an intercultural, interfaith achievement, offering a constructive intellectual demonstration of the way that faith cannot be something which we grasp but which must grasp us; and even further, of the role those of other faiths can play in articulating one's own.[48]

The European Enlightenment further impacted thinking about religious difference. Jean-Jacques Rousseau (1712–78) argued that pluralism was a necessary corollary of democracy. Otherwise, "[i]t is impossible to live at peace with people whom we believe to be damned; to love them would be to hate God who punishes them. It is absolutely necessary to convert them or to punish them."[49]

Christianity's teachings about salvation raise important questions regarding pluralism. Growing out of dynamic and multivocal possibilities, the now familiar doctrine of original sin was framed by Augustine: Adam and Eve's sin in the garden transformed human nature, causing every person to be born in a depraved state, a *massa damnata* (condemned crowd). God's grace is thus required for redemption, possible only through faith in Jesus as Christ, enabling these individuals to attain eternal life. Even this influential teaching, however, did not completely erase Christianity's polyphonic perceptions of God's saving power, particularly in the Eastern Church.

The subsequent question of who is saved tends to obscure the fundamental notion that salvation still represents God's continuing effort toward restoration and reconciliation. Salvation need not focus only on who gets a ticket to heaven. In the Hebrew Bible, it generally refers to *physical* rescue (*yeshua*), available to

---

[47] Nicholas of Cusa, *Nicholas of Cusa on Interreligious Harmony*, 1.2.

[48] Burrell, "Anthropomorphism in Catholic Contexts," 130.

[49] Rousseau, *On the Social Contract*, p. 253.

all, and not all New Testament texts connect it to the afterlife (e.g., Thess 2:13; Eph 1:3–14). Rita Nakashima Brock and Rebecca Ann Parker argue that many Church Fathers considered multiple aspects of "paradise" – material and spiritual, personal and collective, awaited and fulfilled – encompassing the flourishing of God's creation. Themes of communal and historical salvation, traceable within the New Testament and early Christian writings, only slowly gave way to an emphasis on individualized, spiritual possibilities with its stress on the saved and the damned.[50]

While New Testament verses historically understood in exclusivist terms are generally well known, different passages undergird pluralist possibilities. John 3:16–18 tells how "God so loved the world that he gave his only Son" and those who do not believe are condemned. However, God's love can also be conceived in a more universalist way: "Beloved, let us love one another, because love is from God; everyone who loves is born of God and knows God" (1 John 4:7). The First Letter of Paul to Timothy describes God as the "Savior of all people" even as it suggests a preferential standing for those who believe (1 Tim 4:10).

Other verses emphasize righteousness rather than faith. For example, "Not everyone who says to me, 'Lord, Lord,' will enter the kingdom of heaven, but only the one who does the will of my Father in heaven" (Matt 7:21). In addition, concerns about schism in the formation of the Church inspired calls for internal pluralism that contemporary theologians can interpret more broadly. Consider, for example, Paul's focus on love in his epistle to Corinth: "Love is patient; love is kind; love is not envious or boastful or arrogant or rude. It does not insist on its own way; it is not irritable; it keeps no record of wrongs; it does not rejoice in wrongdoing but rejoices in the truth. It bears all things, believes all things, hopes all things, endures all things" (1 Cor 13:4–7; see also Gal 5:22–26).

Such teachings have influenced Christian scholars across the ages to imagine universal salvation. St. Isaac the Syrian (seventh century) asserted that the idea of eternal punishment is incompatible with a loving God and encouraged compassion for all humanity, regardless of faith.[51] Clement of Alexandria, Origen, and Gregory of Nyssa posited that everyone can be restored to friendship with God (*apokatastasis*); punishment may endure for a long time, but God is victorious over sin and death.[52] Even Cyprian's (third century) classic statement *extra ecclesium nulla salus* ("outside of the church, no salvation") did not originally mean to exclude non-Christians from divine grace; it was

---

[50] Brock and Parker, *Saving Paradise*, pp. 84–114.

[51] Isaac the Syrian, *The Wisdom of St. Isaac the Syrian*, loc. 78–88, 307–320.

[52] Gregory of Nyssa, *De Anima et Resurrectione*, p. 46; *Oratia Catechetica*, 26; Clement, *Stromata*, 7:2, 16; Origen, *De Principiis* 3.6.6 (elsewhere he asserted limits). See Acts 3:21; Ramelli, *The Christian Doctrine of* Apokatastasis.

directed as a chastisement to Christians who refused to submit to the bishops' authority.

While the idea of universal salvation enjoyed popularity for a time, many came to believe that it compromised divine justice and the centrality of faith. It was ruled contrary to Church doctrine at the Council of Constantinople in 543. Nonetheless, theological emphasis on a limitlessly loving Christ grew, and there remained a tradition of *apokatastasis* throughout the history of Christian thought – especially among mystics and, more broadly, since the Renaissance.[53]

2.3 Islam

Considerations of multiplicity begin with the Qur'anic text, prompted by critical awareness that there were differences among early written copies. According to a *hadith*, Jibreel told Muhammad that the Qur'an could be recited in only one *harf* (variant or dialect), but the prophet bargained for up to seven. Muslim tradition views this as a divinely intended multiplicity through which Allah conformed the transmission to fit the needs of each community.[54]

Beyond internal polysemy, the Qur'an teaches that there were numerous revelations to diverse peoples throughout history:

> And We have sent down the Book to you with truth, confirming and conserving the previous Books. So judge between them by what Allah has sent down and do not follow their whims and desires deviating from the Truth that has come to you. We have appointed a law and a practice for every one of you. Had Allah willed, He would have made you a single community, but He wanted to test you regarding what has come to you. So compete with each other in doing good. (5:48)

It is a pluralistic notion with a dash of epistemological humility: Live in faithfulness with the covenant you have received. The stated goal is not to prove who is theologically correct, but to demonstrate how your faith leads to right action. In 49:13, another purpose of diversity is identified: so that you may come to know one another (see also 14:4; 2:148).

Each community was elected in its time to accept, embody, and transmit divine instruction – "Every people has a guide" (13:7; see also 10:47; 16:36; 35:24) – acknowledging multiple revelations that overlap but are not identical.

---

[53] Such mystics include Isaac the Syrian, Amalric of Bena (d. ~1207), and Julian of Norwich (d. 1416). Later proponents include Christian universalists dating from seventeenth-century England; see Brock and Parker, *Saving Paradise*, 389–398.

[54] Qadhi, *An Introduction to the Sciences of the Qur'an*, pp. 172–183; Al-Azami, *The History of the Qur'ānic Text*, p. 153. Most academics view *harf* as a textual variant since there are differences in wording, while Muslim tradition considers it a dialect because "variant" suggests uncertainty in transmission.

There is even a notion that the obscure Qur'anic mentions of "Mother of the Book" and "Preserved Tablet" refer to an eternal teaching lodged in Heaven, the framework of primordial religion from which the diverse scriptures were drawn.[55] The words of Allah cannot be exhausted (31:27; 118:109).

Transmitted in the multifaith context of Arabia with some knowledge of Judaism and Christianity as scriptural traditions, the Qur'an repeatedly affirms the validity of the revelations received by Moses, the Hebrew prophets, and Jesus: "We believe in what has been sent down to us and what was sent down to you. Our God and your God are one and we submit to Him" (29:46; see also 2:136; 3:84; 46:12). Although it became common to claim that Jewish and Christian leaders corrupted their scriptures and that Islam is the corrective, in order to justify Islamic supersession (see 2:75; 3:78; 4:46; 5:3), pluralistic possibilities endured. A mystical approach typified by Ibn Arabi (1165–1240) imagined that they were all correct:

> Every sense (*wajh*) which is supported by any verse in God's Speech (*kalam*) – whether it is the Qur'an, the Torah, the Psalms, the Gospel, or the scripture – in the view of anyone who knows that language is intended by God in the case of that interpreter. For His knowledge encompasses all senses. Hence no man of knowledge can declare wrong an interpretation which is supported by the word.[56]

Commenting on a teaching by al-Junayd (ninth to tenth century) that water takes on color from the vessel containing it, which suggests that the shape of a religion depends on context, Ibn Arabi noted that one should not interfere with the beliefs of others. Instead, one should try to "perceive God in every form and in every belief."[57] The Qur'an also insists that there is no compulsion in religion (2:256), a protection of personal conscience that contemporary Islamic scholar Abdulaziz Sachedina called "the major argument for religious pluralism in the Qur'an."[58]

The rapidly expanding Islamic empire absorbed a range of unique cultures, catalyzing broad internal diversity. Custom varied according to place, with veneration of saints in Morocco, pilgrimage to local sacred stones as a substitute for the *hajj* in Southeast Asia, and other heterodox practices.[59] The remarkable variety of Muslim life and thought prompted the eighteenth-century

---

[55] See 3:7; 13:39; 43:4; 85:22. See also Ali and Leaman, *Islam: The Key Concepts*, pp. 102–103.

[56] Ibn Arabi, *The Meccan Revelations* II.119.21, as translated in Shah-Kazemi, "Beyond Polemics and Pluralism: The Universal Message of the Qur'an," in Khalil, *Between Heaven and Hell*, p. 93.

[57] Ibn al'Arabi, *The Bezels of Wisdom*, p. 283.

[58] Sachedina, "The Qur'ān and Other Religions," 294.

[59] Kurzman, "Liberal Islam in Its Islamic Context," in *Liberal Islam*, p. 5. See El Shamsy, "The Social Construction of Orthodoxy," 111–112.

Indian theologian Shah Wali Allah to compose *An Evenhanded Elucidation of the Causes of Disagreement*, "an intellectual history that explained how the single message delivered by the Prophet Muhammad in Arabia had resulted in the stunning plurality and dissonance of the Muslim intellectual landscape."[60]

Amidst this diverse, transnational *ummah*, scripture was clearly used to persuade, coerce, and control – but there remained a developing intrafaith pluralism. Between the first and fourth Islamic centuries, nineteen schools of legal opinion emerged. Even narrowing our focus to the four schools that eventually composed Sunni orthodoxy, Islam's unique approach to multiplicity formalized legal pluralism: All judgments made by qualified jurists and adopted by any of the legal schools were regarded as equally correct. When the Abbasid caliph proposed making Imam Malik's code the single basis for law throughout the empire, the scholar refused, explaining that each region had forged its own path.[61]

As in other traditions, many validations of multiplicity refer only to internal disagreement. Still, the discussions open up space for ambiguity and pluralist thought. Qur'anic exegesis, or *tafsir*, considered one of the Islamic sciences, offers a good example. Interpreters recognized variables such as whether an *ayah* is to be understood literally or metaphorically, applied generally or read narrowly, seen as teaching explicitly or implicitly, in a qualified fashion or unconditionally.[62] The potential to circumscribe exclusivist verses and emphasize more pluralist ones opens up space for difference.

Scholars also identified diverse sources of authority. Both Sunni and Shi'a traditions maintained that the Qur'an and Sunna are the two fundaments for determining Islamic doctrine and practice. Yet methods that rely more on human reason were confirmed and contested to varying degrees, including consensus (*ijma*), juristic discretion (*istihsan*), public interest (*masalih mursalah*), precedent/status quo (*istishab*), and independent reasoning (*ijtihad*), which is generally thought to include analogy (*qiyas*) and personal opinion (*ra'y*).[63] Sufism added inspiration from God to the list, often privileging it over historical tradition.

---

[60] Brown, *Misquoting Muhammad*, p. 16.

[61] Ibn Abdul Barr, *Jāmi' Bayān al-'Ilm* 1/532. See Muhammad Iqbal, "The Principle of Movement in the Structure of Islam" in Kurzman, *Liberal Islam*, p. 263; Rabb, *Doubt in Islamic Law*, p. 204; Brown, *Misquoting Muhammad*, p. 35.

[62] Qadhi, *An Introduction to the Sciences of the Qur'an*, pp. 207–231.

[63] Ahmad Muhammad al-Tayyib, "The Quran as Source of Islamic Law," in Nasr, *The Study Quran*, p. 1717. See also Kamali, *Principles of Islamic Jurisprudence*, pp. 109–156; Ellethy, *Islam, Context, Pluralism and Democracy*.

Certain principles of Islamic law explicitly affirm human authority. Formal obligations commanded in sacred texts are few; for instance, giving adherents the freedom to exercise their autonomous and communal judgments in many matters. A second principle is the "ease of obligations," making exceptions to rules when they are too onerous or when they collide with other values. Human reason is thus required to determine whether circumstances make something lawful that normally would not be (for example, eating during Ramadan because of illness), and when to set aside a command such as "enjoin right and forbid wrong" in order to preserve peace.[64] These precepts empower adherents to define the foundational values of scripture and can serve as an antidote to absolutizing sacred texts.

The human role in ascertaining truth spurred an animated discourse. Islam's concept of *fitra* asserts that Allah endowed humanity with innate capacities for reason and moral cognition. Qur'an 30:30 serves as a prooftext: "Set your face firmly towards the religion as a pure natural believer, Allah's natural pattern (*fitra*) on which He made humanity. There is no changing Allah's creation. That is the true religion, but most people do not know it." If this ethical discernment is independent of revelation, there is more room for religious pluralism. Although most Sunni thinkers, influenced by Asharite theology, denied that human reason can judge right or wrong on its own, Mutazilite and Shi'ite theologians affirmed that it could: Moral agency is a gift and burden that God bestows as an integral element of divine justice.

At the same time, Islamic tradition recognized the limits of human knowledge. As in Judaism and Christianity, Muslim belief embraced God as the Ultimate Absolute, beyond full comprehension by human beings.[65] Mutazilite, Shi'ite, and Sufi Islam emphasized that much of what we affirm about God can be approximated only in the negative – a premise they saw poetically supported by the *shahada*, which begins with a negative/positive assertion: "There is no God but Allah."

Intisar Rabb has written about the essential place of doubt in religious law, explaining that "Muslim jurists collectively *canonized, textualized,* and *generalized* an Islamic doctrine of doubt rooted in early judicial practice." There is foundational doubt, given the fact that there are numerous situations the Qur'an does not address. There is substantive, procedural, and interpretive doubt, fed by textual ambiguity, legal pluralism, and consciousness of historical change. Although Islamic tradition promotes the idea of divine legislative supremacy,

---

[64] Al-Tayyib, "Quran as Source of Islamic Law," 1698–1703.
[65] Nurcholish Madjid, "The Necessity of Renewing Islamic Thought *and* Reinvigorating Religious Understanding," in Kurzman, *Liberal Islam*, 290–291.

the nuance with which medieval Muslim jurists approached that ideal is shrouded in a history not of certainty but of doubt.[66]

Another premodern foundation for pluralist thought within Islam is the tradition of contextualism. One form employs the principle of gradualism. There are three different instructions related to drinking alcohol, for example – a warning that it is sinful (albeit with some benefits, 2:219), a limitation (not to pray while drunk, 4:43), and an outright prohibition (5:90). Rather than view these contradictory verses as an error, they are seen as a mercy, gradually weaning the people from drinking wine.[67] Evoking the notion of accommodation, early works frequently cited the maxim, "We have been commanded to speak to people according to their minds' abilities."[68]

Tradition holds that the Qur'an was revealed to Muhammad over twenty-three years. Since the Qur'an is not presented in chronological order, early Islamic scholars tried to establish the occasions of revelation (*asbab al-nuzul*): What was happening in the world when each passage was taught to Muhammad? The historical contexts they assigned informed interpretations, clarified the relationship of adjacent verses, and grounded the text in the life of the Prophet.[69] The context of revelation did not always limit the message to those particular circumstances, but reflecting on events that gave rise to each prophetic experience aided later believers in appropriately applying the teaching to their own time and place.[70]

Our time and place, with its ever-present diversity and egalitarian principles, has certainly advanced pluralist convictions about religious others – but there are ideas within historical tradition to undergird such values, many embedded in the Qur'an. It speaks plainly of a pluralist peace: "Unto you your religion, and unto me my religion" (109:6), and it recognizes that many People of the Book are upright, pious, and ethical. Like Muslims, they "enjoin the right and forbid the wrong, and compete in doing good. They are among the righteous. You will not be denied the reward for any good thing you do. Allah knows the god-fearing" (3:113–115).

The latter passage gives the impression that faithful observance of other monotheistic traditions may, in fact, be salvific. It certainly applied to biblical figures such as Abraham: "We chose him in this world, and in the Next World he will be one of the righteous" (2:130). Other verses appear to extend the promise

---

[66] Rabb, *Doubt in Islamic Law*, pp. 16, 28, 185–221.

[67] A fourth reference to strong drink describes it as a sign of Allah's generous provision (16:67). See Nasr (ed.), *The Study Quran*, pp. 211–212, 1703.

[68] Brown, *Misquoting Muhammad*, p. 223.   [69] See Rippin, "Occasions of Revelation."

[70] See Wadud, *Qur'an and Woman*, p. 4.

to Jews, Christians, and Sabians in Muhammad's time (5:69; 2:62).[71] Arguing
that all who submit to Allah and do good may receive reward, an early Medinan
sura specifically challenges those Jews or Christians who claim that only one
faith can secure access to paradise (2:111–112).

It is also important to note that being a Muslim does not automatically earn
a spot in the Garden: Divine freedom remains absolute. Allah's grace is
abundant, but there is often a provisional word regarding expectations of
reward: "Obey Allah and the Messenger so that hopefully you will gain
mercy" (3:132; see also 6:155; 28:67; 48:14).

Although several passages position the Muslim community as the new elect,
there are interpretations that question such an assumption. For example, most
commentators understood 5:3 to affirm Islam as the one true path: "This day
I have perfected for you your religion, and completed My Blessing upon you, and
have approved for you as religion, Submission (*Islam*)." They invoked the
principle of *naskh*, in which Allah can annul a teaching and replace it with
something better, to override previous revelations in history. Yet the distinguished
interpreter and historian al-Tabari (838–923) read *islam* here simply as submission of one's heart to the principle of divine Oneness.[72] He carefully collected
exegetical formations of *naskh* that support exclusivist attitudes but rejected their
opinions because he found them incongruent with the divine promise.

Islam's elaborate discursive tradition has tried to preserve the traditional
authority of scripture while also minimizing the dangers of rigidity and absolutism. Commitments to revivification (*tajdid*) and the pursuit of knowledge
have historically included foreign knowledge as well. Islam absorbed Greek
philosophy and understanding of the sciences from the many cultures it encountered. In the early centuries, Muslim scholars collected Jewish, Christian, and
Zoroastrian teachings (generally bundled together as *Isra'iliyyat*) that over-
lapped with Islamic traditions.[73] As one common saying goes, "Foreign knowledge is the lost camel of the believer."[74]

During the Islamic empire's Abbasid caliphate (eighth to thirteenth century),
centered in Baghdad, this culture of engagement led to an early model of
interreligious dialogue. In formal assemblies convened in the court of
a prince, vizier, or caliph, and in more informal salons, diverse religious

---

[71] Traditional exegesis applied such statements only to converts to Islam, but some modern readers
challenge this conclusion. See Sachedina, "The Qur'ān and Other Religions," 296–297; Ayoub,
"Nearest in Amity," 145–164.

[72] See Sachedina, "The Qur'ān and Other Religions," fn. 10; commentary on 5:3 in Nasr (ed.),
Study Quran, p. 276. Cf. 3:85 and commentary there (pp. 153–154).

[73] Later Muslim religious scholars became concerned that the teachings might mislead Muslims
and the literature became discredited.

[74] Moosa, "The Debts and Burdens of Critical Islam," 112.

spokespersons gathered for civil debate and discussion. These *majalis* (councils) promised freedom of expression and respect for all participants, and they were instructed to base their arguments on reason rather than revelation. We also have encyclopedias by Persian scholars al-Biruni (eleventh century) and al-Shahrastani (twelfth century), pioneers in comparative religion, offering sophisticated and respectful treatments of other faiths even as they continued to believe that Islam was superior.[75]

Islamic thought's strong pluralist possibilities are not always recognized in contemporary discourse. The history of colonialism makes it more difficult to reclaim the pluralist voices of Islam's past. They have become tainted with notions of Western influence, even though consideration of textual ambiguity, multivocality, contextuality, and the politics of reading are all native to Islamic tradition. Contemporary Muslim reformers have chosen to engage their religious heritage in its fullest sense, rather than as a synonym for orthodoxy. They embrace what Mohamed Arkoun calls "exhaustive tradition" – the full collection of diverse customs, schools of law, institutions, exegeses, and theologies that are part of their religious inheritance.[76]

2.4 Foundations

Reiterating an essential caveat from Section 1, this is not an exhaustive or balanced record of the traditions. It is a carefully curated collection of teachings to emphasize the pluralist potential within them. All readings of religious thought are selective, so it is important to be transparent about the hermeneutical lens. This assemblage of material makes the following case regarding monotheism and pluralism:

- Historical acceptance of multiplicity makes room for religious differences. While much of it was internally directed, monotheisms have always been able to imagine that God might speak differently to the peoples of the world.
- Long-standing affirmation of the human role in interpreting and embodying revealed teachings should limit the temptation to confuse God's will with our own.
- Ongoing debates about diverse kinds of truth can ground pluralist concepts that different lifestances might all be true in their own ways.
- "Learned ignorance" calls for humility and an embrace of ambiguity. Privileging faith over certainty allows respect for the faiths of others.

---

[75] See Cohen, Griffith, Lazarus-Yafeh, and Somekh (eds.), *The Majlis*; Hilman Latief, "Comparative Religion in Medieval Muslim Literature," 28–62.

[76] Arkoun, "Rethinking Islam Today," in Kurzman, *Liberal Islam*, p. 209.

- Ethical behavior has long been considered a significant metric for God's approval, regardless of lifestance.
- Other contemporary arguments for theological pluralism, including God's overarching love/mercy/power, mutual influence among religions, and freedom of faith, have historical articulations.
- Religious ideas have never "always" meant anything; they have been fluid, multiple, and contested. Historical consciousness argues against privileging one path as if it has infallibly delineated the way for all humanity. The traditional recognition that religions continually change invites us to examine them anew in our twenty-first-century global society.

3 Contemporary Paradigms

Contemporary thinkers who support parity pluralism draw from the historical sources described in Section 2 and adapt teachings of the traditions to our current context. Although the lifestances are distinct and their histories unique, the ways they establish parity often overlap. Consequently, the discussion here is not organized by religion; rather, it identifies various strategies for reading in pluralistic ways, using examples from multiple monotheisms. This method is inclusive but cannot be comprehensive in either depth or breadth. To discover the fullness of individual traditions or the nuance of an individual theologian's approach, there are many published theologies of religions with rigorous analyses where one can turn for deeper study.

Several additional caveats are in order. Parity pluralism sometimes gets presented as the new "highest" understanding of religion, establishing another spiritual hegemony that marginalizes those who do not agree (see Section 4 for further discussion). To avoid that conundrum, this discussion does not try to "prove" that parity is the best or only viewpoint. Parity is not the inevitable conclusion that one can draw from the logics delineated in this sectio. As stated in Section 1.2, the goal is simply to illuminate the space for parity pluralism within monotheistic perspectives.

Also, the categories established by the headings of this section are heuristic. Interpretive strategies overlap, and contemporary scholars work through multiple dimensions of pluralism in their analyses.

Lastly, as explained in Section 1, many scholars have critiqued the exclusivist–inclusivist–pluralist framework, and its original construction around Christian concerns with salvation means that it does not fit other traditions as well. In this work of comparative translation, then, I do not assign a "pluralist" label to the thinkers cited, although many would identify that way. Their arguments simply demonstrate that they are grappling afresh with interpreting religious teachings in light of our current multifaith context.

3.1 Ethics

The driving ethos of pluralism in the modern age is egalitarianism. Most of us know people of other lifestances whom we admire. In our globally connected world with continuous migrations, it goes beyond Mendelssohn's intellectual awareness of a Confucius or a Solon. Individuals who orient around religion differently are also our neighbors, colleagues, friends, and family members.

Parity pluralism seeks to accord respect to other human beings *and* affirm their spiritual choices. It maintains that we should see our faith as contributing to the world's store of sacred wisdom rather than owning it. From a parity perspective, true equity and respect seem impossible when others' spiritual truths are dismissed as inferior or subordinate; a hierarchy of lifestances establishes a hierarchy of humanity. As the French historian and philosopher Michel Foucault persuasively demonstrated, truth claims readily become power claims.[77]

History makes evident how theological exclusivism can justify and perpetuate domination. European colonialism presents a classic example: "The moral validation of the imperial enterprise rested upon the conviction that it was a great civilizing and uplifting mission, one of whose tasks was to draw the unfortunate heathen up into the higher, indeed highest, religion of Christianity. Accordingly, the gospel played a vital role in the self-justification of Western imperialism."[78]

Claims of theological ultimacy also link to other hierarchies regarding gender, sexual orientation, and race, multiplying conflict with the ethics of equality. Even people who reject parity pluralism are influenced by these social realities and pressed to address these concerns.[79]

In contemporary interreligious dialogue, parity pluralism often grows from the transformative impact of encounter. A number of pioneers in the field did not begin their journeys as pluralists, but respect for their dialogue partners grew, as did their appreciation for the beauty and wisdom found in other faiths. They subsequently sought theological foundations for parity. Prominent Christian examples include Wilfred Cantwell Smith, Raimon Panikkar, John Hick,

---

[77] See, for example, Foucault, *Power/Knowledge*.

[78] John Hick, "The Non-Absoluteness of Christianity," in Hick and Knitter, *The Myth of Christian Uniqueness*, p. 19.

[79] See, for example, Timothy Winter, "Realism and the Real," in Khalil, *Between Heaven and Hell*, pp. 141–143.

Rosemary Radford Ruether, and Leonard Swidler.[80] Rabbi Zalman Schachter-Shalomi, raised within the Lubavitcher tradition, and Shi'ite scholar Hasan Askari traversed similar arcs.[81] Comparative theologians have remarked that this sequence is preferred; we should seek to understand one another through encounters rather than explain one another through theologies of religion. Francis Clooney, for example, asserts, "The comparative theologian can be in conversation with other theologians about basic truths and how they are to be understood after comparative learning is well underway."[82]

The ethical impetus toward pluralism reflects the desire to exorcise religious sources of human oppression that can flow from claims of supremacy or supersession, but it is also deeply rooted in religious teachings of equality. Islam's concept of *fitra* asserts that all humans are born with a purity of soul and a capacity to recognize both God and goodness. Abdulaziz Sachedina reasoned that this presses us toward parity in our desire to deal with one another equitably.[83] The Hebrew Bible's charge to "love your neighbor as yourself" (Lev 19:18, cited in Matt 22:39) can be interpreted to mean that, among other things, your neighbor's lifestance is to be honored as we would expect our own to be. The basic value of reciprocity – the golden rule – is found in almost every lifestance.

The deepest insight of pluralism, according to Irving Greenberg, a modern orthodox rabbi, is that "dignity, truth and power function best when they are pluralized, e.g., divided and distributed, rather than centralized or absolutized."[84] He argues that pluralism is not relativism; pluralists are not required to forfeit the idea that there is an ultimate truth. However, disagreement requires that people of faith practice self-restraint and self-criticism. Assertions of absolutism lead to devaluing other human beings. Catholic theologian Anselm Kyongsuk Min expresses this conviction as dialectical confessional pluralism. Privileging the commitment to promote the well-being of all, living together in peace, he maintains that people must examine the impact of their truth claims and adapt them to advance solidarity.[85]

Most people assign degrees of parity, even if we do so subconsciously. We naturally prefer our own lifestance and perhaps see it as the medieval Muslim scholar Ibn Arabi saw Islam: Ours is the light of the sun, and other traditions illuminate in lesser ways, like the moon and the stars. Those that are close to us

---

[80] Schmidt-Leukel, *Religious Pluralism and Interreligious Theology*, chap. 2.

[81] See Schachter-Shalomi, "No Other," 21–24; Siddiqui, *Christian-Muslim Dialogue in the Twentieth Century*, pp. 110–111.

[82] Clooney, *Comparative Theology*, p. 16.

[83] Sachedina, "The Qur'ān and Other Religions," p. 297.

[84] Greenberg, *For the Sake of Heaven and Earth*, p. 201.

[85] Min, "Dialectical Pluralism and Solidarity of Others," 587–604.

shine a bit brighter. By identifying these as personal judgments rather than objective universal claims, however, the ethics of parity can be maintained. Reform Rabbi Arnold Jacob Wolf (1924–2008) offers the analogy to marriage: We do not need to assert that our spouse is the most exceptional person in the world – only that they are the right person for us, the one who makes us better, the one who teaches us to love, the one who makes us whole. Besides, Wolf notes, we cannot really know what someone else's spouse (or faith) is like without the intimacy of a life together.[86]

Ethical arguments for parity do not require that we abstain from judgment altogether. Instead, they frame the criteria in ethical measure. Khaled Abou El Fadl, a scholar of Islamic law, notes that the Qur'an identifies justice as the highest moral virtue (4:135).[87] Theologians Marjorie Hewitt Suchocki (United Methodist) and Paul Knitter (Buddhist Catholic) assert that working toward the inclusive well-being of humanity is the fundamental criterion of value, and religions are true insofar as they orient people toward justice and liberation.[88] John Hick (1922–2012), a pioneering Christian voice for theological pluralism, advocates assessing lifestances by their capacity to cultivate "fruits of the spirit" (Gal 5:22–23), especially love (in Koine Greek, *agape*) and compassion (in Sanskrit, *karuṇā*).[89]

This metric echoes the rabbinic conviction that righteous people of all faiths participate in the blessings of "the next world," and the Qur'anic instruction that communities of faith should compete with each other in doing good (2:148). Regarding the latter, South African Muslim scholar Farid Esack suggests that we should "proselytize" – not to convert the world to our faith but collectively to establish "liberative praxis aimed at creating a world of socio-economic and gender justice where all human beings are free to explore and attain their unique fullness, intended with their creation."[90] Ethics are themselves culturally constructed, of course, but nonideological dialogue facilitates critical exploration of our respective norms.

An emphasis on ethics also demands that we reexamine the ways in which difference has historically been understood. Feminist and womanist hermeneutics, acutely conscious of how power is deployed to determine which differences matter and what they mean, have been helpful in this endeavor. In a *Muslima* theology of religious pluralism, for instance, Professor of Islam and Interreligious Engagement Jerusha Rhodes reviews all the relevant Qur'anic

---

[86] Wolf, "The State of Jewish Belief."

[87] Abou El Fadl, in Cohen and Lague (eds.), *The Place of Tolerance in Islam*, pp. 14–16.

[88] See their respective contributions to Hick and Knitter (eds.), *The Myth of Christian Uniqueness*.

[89] Hick, *An Interpretation of Religion*, pp. 325–327.

[90] Esack, "Muslims Engaging the Other and the Humanum," 529.

verses and identifies a range of dynamic, overlapping categories that yield a more complex reading of difference in the Muslim tradition. The terms include *mu'min, muslim, mushrik, kafir, ahl al-kitab, munafiq,* and *ḥanif* – commonly translated, respectively, as believer, submitter, associator, disbeliever, People of the Book, hypocrite, and [nondenominational] monotheist. She concludes that all claims of divine favor based on membership in an essentialized "religion" are suspect. Noting that Qur'anic descriptions of religious difference are quickly followed by exhortations to manifest *taqwa* (God-consciousness), Rhodes argues that the Qur'an is not primarily a verdict on religious difference but a guide to God consciousness and proper behavior.[91] Her deconstruction of historical assumptions about religious difference demonstrates one way to recover pluralist possibilities.

3.2 The Nature of the Divine

Many theologians see parity pluralism as the natural and necessary implication of divine love. The idea of limiting its fullness or its salvific potential to a single path seems improbable, even immoral. How can people leading worthy lives be doomed for belonging to a different religion, particularly since membership in a religious community is largely a matter of circumstance – dependent on one's time, place, and family of origin? Faith in a just and loving God cannot accept that human redemption should depend on such randomness.[92]

Even imagining that the "non-elect" are somehow marginal to divine purposes challenges faith in a loving God. Greenberg writes about Jewish chosenness in a way that both recognizes God's universal love and celebrates particularity: "God's love – God's redemptive love – which is the basis of chosenness, is never the monopoly of any one people. ... That cannot take away my unique experience or my feeling of uniqueness."[93]

Divine power is also implicated. As philosopher William Chittick notes, not only does Allah's all-embracing mercy make it impossible to imagine that God wants most of humanity to suffer in inescapable darkness but also if God intended the whole world to be one religion, divine omnipotence suggests it should have come to pass already. "If Islam – or any other religion – were the unique saving message, then God would turn out to have been totally incompetent."[94]

---

[91] Lamptey (now Rhodes), *Never Wholly Other*, chaps. 6–8.
[92] Sagi, "Justifying Interreligious Pluralism," in Goshen-Gottstein and Korn, *Jewish Theology and World Religions*, p. 62.
[93] Greenberg, *Living in the Image of God*, p. 79.
[94] Chittick, "The Ambiguity of the Qur'anic Command," in Khalil, *Between Heaven and Hell*, p. 84.

Monotheism's belief in God's limitless capacity additionally prompts arguments that no tradition can exhaust the fullness of divine truth. Turkish scholar Mahmut Aydin affirms the universal significance of the Qur'an while maintaining that the divine may be revealed in other ways as well.[95] Catholic theologian Stephen Duffy makes a similar claim regarding Jesus:

> Christianity's central affirmation, that divine Wisdom is incarnate in Jesus, ought not be construed to mean that Jesus is the sole medium in which God's creative and reconciling agency may be present in the world. No understanding of the religions is acceptable that denies the love of God for all creation or holds hostage in one small corner of the world the power of God to overcome the alienation of humanity from its ground.[96]

Both Duffy and Rabbi Abraham Joshua Heschel argue that it is idolatrous to see one's own perspective as the whole of the story. "Does not the all-inclusiveness of God contradict the exclusiveness of any particular religion?" asks Heschel. "Is it not blasphemous to say: I alone have all the truth and the grace?"[97]

Christian theology presents another dimension of God's nature that supports pluralist thought: There is an abiding multiplicity within God's own being. Those who reject parity still recognize that the Trinity establishes relational reciprocity as the very nature of God.[98] Parity pluralists take it further. Director of Harvard's Pluralism Project, Diana Eck writes: "From a Christian pluralist standpoint, the multiplicity of religious ways is a concomitant of the ultimacy and many-sidedness of God, the one who cannot be limited or encircled by any one tradition."[99] Each religion realizes a vital aspect of the divine, and the fullness of God is revealed not by suppressing or overcoming differences but by living into them. For several Christian thinkers, this capaciousness is particularly fostered by the Holy Spirit, which rests on both those who believe in Jesus as Christ and those who do not. Humans are perpetually pulled to the transcendent, drawn to the Spirit through difference in what the author of Ephesians calls the multicolored wisdom of God (3:10).[100] According to Jacques Dupuis, a Jesuit priest and theologian, Trinitarian theology makes it possible to see religious diversity as a gift from God – a superabundance of divine manifestations to humanity.[101]

---

[95] Aydin, "Islam in a World of Diverse Faiths—A Muslim View," 33–54.

[96] Duffy, "The Stranger within Our Gates: Interreligious Dialogue and the Normativeness of Jesus," in Merrigan and Haers, *The Myriad Christ*, 4–5.

[97] Heschel, "No Religion Is an Island," 126.

[98] Markofski, "Reflexive Evangelicalism," 47–74.   [99] Eck, *Encountering God*, p. 186.

[100] See Suchocki, *Divinity and Diversity*; Peter C. Hodgson, "The Spirit and Religious Pluralism," in Knitter, *Myth of Religious Superiority*, 135–150.

[101] Dupuis, "Trinitarian Christology as a Model for a Theology of Religious Pluralism," in Merrigan and Haers, *The Myriad Christ*, p. 96.

Several contemporary theological constructs posit additional characteristics of the divine that align with parity pluralism. Phenomenological approaches note that the riotous diversity of creation anticipates and affirms the multiplicity of religious experience. Process theology asserts that change is ontologically funda-mental even in God, operating in a co-creative relationship – implicitly arguing against a static universal "true" faith. Reconstructionist Rabbi Toba Spitzer, for example, interprets Torah's narrative at the burning bush, where God claims the name *Ehyeh asher ehyeh*, "I will be what I will be" (Exod 3:14), as

> [a] kind of biblical proof text for Whitehead's contention that God is the ultimate Source of all possibility and potentiality in the universe. . . . The God of the Torah, and the God of our daily experience of the world, is not an abstract, unchanging, and immutable Unmoved Mover, but That which allows the universe to unfold in all of its dazzling complexity.[102]

Christian theologian Catherine Keller draws similar conclusions from the cre-ation narrative, seeing the "face of the deep" as representative of an irreducible multiplicity in creation. Reading the Genesis 1 narrative closely, she identifies the process of creation as invitation and cooperation: "let us make . . . " – suggesting a relatedness and interdependency that permeate existence, a process of becoming through the foundational synergy of difference.[103]

Liberation theology's emphasis on God's preference for the poor often leads its advocates to hold that the poor are God's people regardless of religious affiliation.[104] Womanist theology similarly concludes that love cannot be sep-arate from inclusive justice. As Emilie Townes, a Christian social ethicist and theologian, writes, "God's love moves out to grow in compassion, understand-ing, and acceptance of one another. It helps begin the formation of a divine – human community based on love that is pointed toward justice."[105]

Divine love, power, limitlessness, many-sidedness, relationality, dynamism, and commitment to human liberation – all these qualities can be drawn upon to support monotheistic approaches to parity pluralism.

3.3 Divinely Intended Difference

Many pluralist paradigms argue that if God is indeed benevolent and powerful as monotheisms generally assert, then the multitude of spiritual lifestances must be divinely intended. "The diversity of humankind is not the result of the

---

[102] Spitzer, "Why We Need Process Theology," 89.   [103] Keller, *The Face of the Deep*, p. 195.
[104] See Paul F. Knitter, "Toward a Liberation Theology of Religions," in Hick and Knitter, *Myth of Christian Uniqueness*, pp. 178–218; Cascante-Gómez, "Latin American Theology and Religious Pluralism," 556–563.
[105] Townes, *In a Blaze of Glory*, p. 140.

degeneration of human society or the lack of divine guidance; it is, rather, the very will of God," wrote Mahmut Aydin, validated by Qur'anic verses that identify Allah's purpose in religious diversity as competing with each other to do good (5:48), or coming to know one another (49:13).[106]

The biblical story of the Tower of Babel (Gen 11:1–9) advances a similar argument. Interpreting the dispersion as a rejection of the builders' imperial monoculture, orthodox Rabbi Jonathan Sacks (1948–2020) argued that it is a correction rather than a punishment or an etiology of cultural diffusion and conflict. The tower, with its unitary worldview and objective, runs counter to the natural proliferation of languages, cultures, and peoples described in the preceding section of Genesis. So God reestablishes difference. At the conclusion of the tale, the Hebrew Bible begins the story of *one* people in a relationship with its God in a world of plural particularities.[107]

Another orthodox Jewish scholar, David Hartman, maintains that revelation is never meant to be universal but particular and specific – an assertion of several medieval thinkers mentioned in Section 2 and growing more common today. Revelation is not intended to be the source of absolute, universal, and eternal truth. Rather, it is God speaking to human beings within the limited framework of human language and specific cultural contexts, building communities of faith within history.[108]

A common suggestion is that God desires a religiously diverse world because the multitude of human spiritualities exist in productive tension and symbiosis. We know that sustainable ecosystems require diversity to thrive – a biological fact that can apply to intellectual and spiritual life as well. Engagement with difference is essential to the fullest development of our respective religions and individual selves; it expands our grasp of complexity and capacity to adapt. As biblical scholar Claus Westermann wrote in his commentary on Genesis (12:36), "The stranger comes from another world and has a message from it."[109]

Drawing from John Cobb, a prominent scholar of process theology, this conviction can be termed complementary pluralism. The task of theological dialogue, then, is to help one another achieve our spiritual goals.[110] Participants in interreligious dialogue and comparative theology repeatedly testify to this experience: Encounter with difference deepens their understanding of their own

---

[106] Aydin, "A Muslim Pluralist: Jalaluddin Rûmi," in Hick and Knitter, *Myth of Religious Superiority*, p. 44. See also Ashgar Ali Engineer, "Islam and Pluralism," in the same volume, 212–213; Sachedina, "The Qur'ān and Other Religions," 305; Mun'im Sirry, "'Compete with One Another in Good Works,'" 424–438.

[107] Sacks, *The Dignity of Difference*, pp. 50–56. See also Panikkar, *Invisible Harmony*, pp. 53–55.

[108] Hartman, *Conflicting Visions*, pp. 247–249.   [109] Westermann, *Genesis 12–36*, p. 277.

[110] David Ray Griffin, "John Cobb's Whiteheadian Complementary Pluralism," in Griffin, *Deep Religious Pluralism*, 39–66.

lifestance in a coformative process. In *I and Thou*, Jewish philosopher Martin Buber (1878–1965) proposed that we can engage with all of creation, not only human beings, in ways that transcend utilitarian experience and objectification. In place of an "I–It" relationship, we seek out the fullness of the other in intersubjective meeting: "I–Thou." Buber also asserted that we become our complete, actualized selves only by means of such I–Thou relationships: "[A person] becomes an I through a You." To Buber, "all actual life is encounter."[111] It is an evocative framework for considering the profound implications of our codependent existence and spiritual development.

Moving beyond interpersonal impact, Marjorie Suchocki writes about the "call and response" of creation and revelation, with God working in unique ways with communities throughout history: "[T]he peoples of the earth are being called by God to become a community of friends. Diversity, rather than being a hindrance to unity, is instead absolutely necessary for deepest community."[112] This is the "richer unity" that the Qur'an urges, according to Muslim liberation theologian Ashgar Ali Engineer, extolled as the natural result of positive engagement with diversity.[113]

Religions have relevance for each other despite their irreducible differences.[114] They have always learned, borrowed from one another, and changed over time. Many feminist perspectives highlight this dimension of religious plurality. Jerusha Rhodes' book title, *Never Wholly Other*, emphasizes how diverse traditions and communities are bound together; we are essential to each other's formation. Constructive theologian Jeannine Hill Fletcher points out that the impasse of sameness and difference in standard Christian approaches to theology of religions fails to account for meaningful interaction and influence. Religions are not static, homogeneous, or hermetically sealed; they continually develop in encounter with different lifestances.[115]

Professor of Religious Studies and Intercultural Theology, Perry Schmidt-Leukel has borrowed from mathematics to introduce fractal theory into theology, observing that the diversity we find among religions is mirrored in variations within each tradition, in shifting scales. Discernible patterns lead him to explore the possibility of interreligious theology, drawing on multiple traditions to illuminate questions of our existence.[116]

While we learn from one another, and the dialectical energies of our differences can hone our understanding, the object is not to dissolve distinct

---

[111] Buber, *I and Thou*, pp. 80, 62.   [112] Suchocki, *Divinity and Diversity*, pp. 18, 22.

[113] Engineer, "Islam and Pluralism," in Hick and Knitter, *Myth of Religious Superiority*, p. 42.

[114] Cornille, *Im-Possibility of Interreligious Dialogue*, p. 95.

[115] Fletcher, *Monopoly on Salvation? A Feminist Approach to Religious Pluralism*.

[116] Schmidt-Leukel, *Religious Pluralism and Interreligious Dialogue*, chap. 14.

lifestances into some new universal truth – as opponents of religious pluralism sometimes suggest. Yet the question of truth is significant. The contemporary strategies discussed so far begin with the "why" of parity, but we have not yet addressed the particular challenges of revealed religions regarding truth. How can cosmic and acosmic, theist and nontheist lifestances all be true in a monotheistic worldview – and how can they be of comparable value if some are false? The following three strategies focus on the "how" of parity with competing truth claims.

3.4 Convergence

Perennial philosophy, richly expounded by Frithjof Schuon (1907–98) and popularized by Aldous Huxley (1894–1963), maintains that there is a unified reality or Godhead at the core of the world's religions. The *ein sof* (a reference to God, literally "without end") of Jewish mysticism, the *atman-brahman* of Hinduism, the *dharmakāya* of Mahayana Buddhism, the *Dao* (way), and so on, all grasp some transcendental element of a universal metaphysical truth.[117]

John Hick was a key figure in excavating the theological significance of this perspective and called for a "Copernican revolution" in Christian thought about religious pluralism:

> Now the Copernican revolution in astronomy consisted in a transformation in the way in which men understood the universe and their own location within it. It involved a shift from the dogma that the earth is the centre of the revolving universe to the realisation that it is the sun that is at the centre, with all the planets, including our own earth, moving around it. And the needed Copernican revolution in theology involves an equally radical transformation in our conception of the universe of faiths and the place of our own religion within it. It involves a shift from the dogma that Christianity is at the centre to the realisation that it is *God* who is at the centre, and that all the religions of mankind, including our own, serve and revolve around him.[118]

In a series of lectures and writings, he argued that different religions reflect different experiences of the same divine reality – naming it as "the Real" in part to account for nontheistic lifestances. He adapted Immanuel Kant's distinction between *noumena* (things as they are) and *phenomena* (things as they appear) and maintained that we cannot know the Real *an sich* (in itself). Instead, we perceive partial, finite aspects – accounting for the differences between lifestances. Shared values and grammars among diverse spiritual orientations

---

[117] Huxley, *The Perennial Philosophy.*

[118] Hick, *God and the Universe of Faiths*, pp. 130–131. One assumes that, had his work been published slightly later, he would also have recognized the need to utilize gender-inclusive language.

support the hypothesis that they are drawn from a single source; apparent contradictions simply highlight the fathomless depths of the Real.[119]

This approach is sometimes identified as "reductive pluralism," embedding a critique that it fails to recognize substantive differences between lifestances or subsumes them in a comprehensive theory of religion that distorts their essence (see Section 4 for further discussion). Here, we use the more neutral terms "convergent" or "identist" pluralism, signifying the conviction that the various religions are interacting with and pointing toward (identifying, *not* identical) the same transcendent reality.[120]

A popular articulation is that religions constitute "different roads up the same mountain," but this oversimplification is particularly susceptible to charges of relativism. It effaces differences that matter and does not capture the complexity of convergent pluralism. First, not all religious teachings lead *up*; parity pluralism does not forfeit the critical capacity to grapple with harm inflicted in the name of God. Second, scholars have provided conceptual tools to address concerns about conflicting truth claims.

Shi'ite scholar Seyyed Hossein Nasr, for example, imagines religions as distinct solar systems – reviving premodern metaphysics "to see each religion as a religion and *the* religion, 'absolute' within its own universe, while reconfirming that ultimately only the Absolute is absolute." Drawing a distinction between the exoteric forms of religion and their inner, unified essence, he maintains that "the multiplicity of sacred forms [are] not contradictions which relativize, but a confirmation of the universality of the Truth and the infinite creative power of the Real that unfolds Its inexhaustible possibilities in worlds of meaning which, although different, all reflect the unique Truth."[121]

As Nasr indicates, identism can draw from traditional sources. The Qur'an teaches that Allah "has prescribed for you as religion that which He enjoined upon Noah, and that which We revealed unto thee, and that which We enjoined upon Abraham, Moses, and Jesus, that you uphold religion and not become divided therein" (42:13). In New Testament, Paul's comment that "now we see only a reflection, as in a mirror" (1 Cor 13:12), with clarity available to us in some unnamed future, presages the distinction between *noumena* and *phenomena*.

Philo (c. 20 BCE–50 CE) put Judaism in conversation with Hellenistic philosophy, identifying as "Israel" all those who pursue knowledge of God through a philosophical quest. He maintained that the Torah accorded with the best teachings of righteousness among the nations, yet it was also a particular

---

[119] Hick, *An Interpretation of Religion.*

[120] See Griffin, "Religious Pluralism: Generic, Identist, and Deep," in *Deep Religious Pluralism,* p. 24.

[121] Nasr, *Knowledge and the Sacred,* p. 281.

expression as revealed to and embodied by the Jewish people.[122] Philo's claim that transcendent unity and particular differences are inextricably bound together is broadly similar to that of Hasan Askari, a contemporary Muslim scholar: "By 'islam' (primordial and universal) the particular and the historical Islam is abolished. But what is in principle abolished is not in historical fact annulled: the abolition of the particular by the universal has to be enacted within the practice of the particular."[123]

Mirroring the conviction of perennial philosophy that all religious experience is a reflection of the One singular reality of the universe, mystical expressions of various lifestances set unity within diversity at the core of their metaphysics. Sufism speaks of *wahdat al-wujud*, the Unity of Being, in which only God truly exists. The world of ideas and things is but a fleeting shadow, reflecting a partial, temporary self-disclosure of Allah. The Jewish mystical tradition of Kabbalah has a related premise: All of existence unfolds through the *sefirot*, a series of emanations of the divine. All of existence is but a reflection of God, including our differences.

Hasidism is another Jewish orientation infused with mysticism. Alon Goshen-Gottstein summarizes Rabbi Arthur Green's neo-Hasidic theology, noting that it

> points from relative truth to absolute or higher truth, from truth in its diversity to truth in a unified sense, from the multiple and conflicting truths of conflicting narratives and practices to the unified truth that the mystic accesses and wherein he encounters mystics of other traditions as partakers of the same truth. According to this construct, the internal core of all religions is one, and it is here that religions meet. This is the real truth, to which the scaffolding of religion is but a preparation.[124]

As partial expressions of a greater reality, it is possible to affirm the comparable validity of multiple lifestances. Yet in suggesting a certain incompleteness or insufficiency for all of them, this pluralist strategy overlaps with the next, which emphasizes the limits of human understanding.

3.5 Limits of Human Understanding

The notion of epistemological limits is not a recent innovation. Every rigorous analysis of learning has bumped up against the boundaries of human cognition, and religious discourse has taken this constraint to heart. As discussed in Section 2, Augustine and Nicholas of Cusa spoke of "learned ignorance,"

---

[122] Berkowitz, *Defining Jewish Difference*, pp. 41–59.

[123] Askari, "Within and Beyond the Experience of Religious Diversity," 199.

[124] Goshen-Gottstein, *Religious Truth*, pp. 15–16.

valorizing the admission of all we cannot know – especially when it comes to the nature of God. The Qur'an distinguishes between the inexhaustible word of God in the "Preserved Tablet" lodged in heaven, and the revelation sent down to the earth as an utterable fragment.[125] From *via negativa* – the assertion that we can at best say what God is not, found among numerous Christian and Jewish thinkers – to Islam's teaching that we must wait for God to reveal the ultimate truth about areas of disagreement (*irja*), theologians have repeatedly emphasized our limited understanding. Truth may be absolute and even singular, but we do not hold its fullness in our hands.

Contemporary scholars build on these foundations in various ways, including individuals who do not necessarily consider themselves parity pluralists. Tariq Ramadan evokes *irja* without using the term when he writes: "With the acknowledgement that there is a judgment that is beyond our understanding ... we are protected from any dogmatic positioning. The unknown with salvation is a spiritual, living school of humility: to learn to believe firmly in our truth and, in the very name of that truth, to respect Others' way toward the truth."[126]

Lauren Smelser White invokes *kenosis*, Jesus' self-emptying act, as a model for comparative theology and interreligious dialogue: "We cease to assert preemptive epistemological rights over our religious neighbors and thus should expect to be surprised – and even informed – by the epistemic assertions about transcendent reality that we find in the neighboring text."[127]

This strategy fits well with more "orthodox" positions because it allows for the assertion of a single divine truth, even though it is always imperfectly mediated by human beings. As Raphael Jospe quips, drawing from an insight of the medieval Jewish scholar Abraham ibn Ezra, "The problem of revelation is not what is spoken, but what is heard."[128]

The strategy is significant for parity pluralists because it makes room for lifestances that do not affirm parity as long as they resist religions' self-absolutizing inclinations. The premise is that diverse lifestances each capture something invaluable, but none can claim exhaustive authority, exclusive knowledge, or comprehensive understanding. Religious traditions are designed to cultivate faith, not certainty; their truths are truths to live by rather than absolutes. With our partial and provisional understanding, ambiguity liberates us from worrying that those who do not agree with us are intellectually or

---

[125] Arkoun, *The Unthought in Contemporary Islamic Thought*, p. 74.

[126] Ramadan, "Salvation—The Known and the Unknown," in Khalil, *Between Heaven and Hell*, p. xiii.

[127] White, "For Comparative Theology's Christian Skeptics," 175.

[128] Jospe, "Pluralism out of the Sources of Judaism," in Goshen-Gottstein and Korn, *Jewish Theology and World Religions*, p. 105.

morally deficient. We may not be climbing the same mountain, but we are all still mid-journey.

Abraham Joshua Heschel maintains that the most urgent catalyst for engaging those who orient around religion differently is that our deepest experiences of faith reveal themselves to be "mere waves in the endless ocean of mankind's reaching out for God, where all formulations and articulations appear as understatements," and we become acutely aware of the tragic insufficiency of our grasp.[129]

The limits of human understanding are also evident when we remember that religions are perpetually changing, complex organisms amidst dynamic historical processes. They are human constructions, attempts to interpret and bear witness to our perceptions of the transcendent. For those who affirm that sacred texts themselves are authored by human beings as dimensions of that witness, absolutist claims about scriptural truth are automatically diffused. God does not reveal a religion, but rather the divine self.[130]

At the same time, epistemological humility does not negate the value of religious teachings. Drawing on Rumi and Hafez, Iranian philosopher Abdulkarim Soroush concedes that human knowledge is always tentative and imperfect, but he discerns an evolution toward truth. "Instead of seeing the world as consisting of one straight line plus hundreds of crooked and broken lines," we should "see it as consisting of an aggregate of straight lines which meet, run parallel and overlap: truths immersed within truths." He identifies the Qur'an's repeating affirmation that Allah guided various religious figures along *a* straight path (not *the* straight path) as substantiating his conviction.[131]

While epistemological humility is a long-standing dimension of religious thought, contemporary discourse adds the insights of postmodernism, including awareness that all knowledge is situated knowledge. Multiple lifestances reflect multiple culturally conditioned interpretations of ultimate reality. It can be considered a kind of hermeneutical pluralism, drawing on the work of Heidegger, Ricoeur, and Gadamer. "Gadamer uses the term "horizon" to designate the position from which the interpreter approaches the text (or other object of interpretation). One's horizon is constituted by one's present phenomenal and conceptual environment as well as the history that has shaped this present and the particular ways in which one is open toward future possibilities."[132]

---

[129] Heschel, "No Religion Is an Island," p. 122.
[130] See, e.g., Smith, *Towards a World Theology*, p. 33; Smith, *The Meaning and End of Religion*, p. 129.
[131] Soroush, *The Expansion of Prophetic Experience*, p. 136.
[132] Norton, "Religious Pluralism."

Hermeneutical pluralism denies the possibility of objective access to truth, but it is not necessarily an unfortunate limitation. It preserves the space of difference and becomes, in Reform Jewish theologian Dan Cohn-Sherbok's term, a model of pursuing "truth-through-relationship."[133] Paul Knitter offers the image of religions as telescopes, enabling us to see in profound and essential ways, but not everything. Our view is enhanced through conversation with those who look through other telescopes.[134]

3.6 The Plurality of Truth

Most contemporary articulations of parity take the enduring reality of difference as their starting point. Raimon Panikkar, a Roman Catholic priest of Spanish/ Catholic and Indian/Hindu heritage, offers the image of rivers flowing in diverse regions of the earth and yielding life-giving waters to those who drink from them. The rivers never meet on earth, but they do in the heavens, transformed into vapor or spirit, and then rain down again on all creation. The metaphor seeks to substantiate the abiding uniqueness of each lifestance, imagining their interrelatedness without essentializing them. Panikkar believes truth itself is plural.[135]

Such a concept may seem illogical, but Plato, with his world of forms where what is real and true must be universal and timeless, represents only one school of thought. It became dominant in the wake of Immanuel Kant, who tied the principle to morality as well. These two giants of the Western philosophical tradition helped to shape Enlightenment notions that goodness, ethics, and truth must be universal.

Yet, philosophy, both ancient and modern, has grappled with the plural nature of truth. Heraclitus (sixth century BCE) wrote about the unity of opposites. The Chinese school of Yinyang taught that apparently opposing forces are, in fact, complementary, and harmony between them contributes to the vital force (*qi*) of the universe. Abu'l Fadl (1551–1602), a court philosopher under the Mughal emperor Akbar, professed that truth is the inhabitant of every place; the sages themselves are evidence that it cannot be confined to one religion. Hegel critiqued Kant for ignoring how plurality and contradiction lead to understanding; everything involves a coexistence of opposed elements.[136]

---

[133] Cohn-Sherbok, *Judaism and Other Faiths*, p. 160.

[134] Knitter, *Introducing Theologies of Religions*, pp. 11–12.

[135] Panikkar, *A Dwelling Place for Wisdom*, pp. 112–114, 146–147.

[136] See Daniel W. Graham, "Heraclitus" and Robin R. Wang, "Yinyang," *Internet Encyclopedia of Philosophy*; Shah-Kazemi, *The Spirit of Tolerance in Islam*, pp. 35–36; Hegel, *Encyclopaedia of the Philosophical Sciences*, Part 1: B.2.48.

What then can we say about religious truth? John Cobb, Raphael Jospe, Raimon Panikkar, and others have challenged the assumption that ultimate reality is singular rather than irreducibly plural. Jospe writes: "There is, at least as yet, no "unified theory" combining quantum mechanics on the sub-atomic level, and gravity on the astronomic level of general relativity. If, then, we are forced to acknowledge fundamental uncertainty in physics, how can we continue to insist on certainty and absolute truth in metaphysics?" Consequently, he affirms that diverse lifestances have intrinsic value as unique elements within that complexity.[137]

Truth also has different measures and meanings depending on the subject and context. Let's start with the semantic difference between "true friend" and "true story." To be judged true, observations need to be verified, mathematics requires formulaic proof, and moral principles must cohere with a body of convictions. Professor of Jewish philosophy, Tamar Ross, summarizing the work of Rabbi Abraham Isaac Kook, argues that there is a tension between truth as a statement and truth as a dimension of one's being. The value of some truth claims is not that they capture ultimate reality, but that they shape the person and lead them toward a higher state of being.[138] Consider also the dialectical insight that there are often competing truths, such as the need for stability and the need for change, requiring us to navigate the tension between them. These reflections only begin to illuminate how truths are of diverse kinds. Spiritual lifestances deal in multiple types of truth, sometimes so diverse that "true" does not best describe their purpose.

Another formulation speaks about the pluralism of religious ends, with each lifestance uniquely well-adapted in pursuit of its identified goals. Christian theologian S. Mark Heim has written, "We can avoid the stale deadlock of the instrumental question over what will get you there – 'One way or many ways?' – by asking with real openness, 'Way to what?'"[139] This approach is not as tidy as one might wish: Buddhism, Sikhism, Jainism, and Hindu traditions all pursue *nirvana*, for example, but identify the path and the purpose differently. These lifestances have a long history of debate and discernment that makes clear the "way to what" can still be contested.

Nonetheless, the pluralism of religious ends helps to establish parity by acknowledging that each lifestance has an internal coherence and value. With a superfluity of conflicting testimony, discrete pockets of evidence support

---

[137] Jospe, "Pluralism Out of the Sources of Judaism," in Goshen-Gottstein and Korn, *Jewish Theology and World Religions*, p. 119.

[138] Ross, "The Cognitive Value of Religious Truth Statements: Rabbi A. I. Kook and Postmodernism," in Goshen-Gottstein, *Religious Truth*, pp. 133–176.

[139] Heim, "Dreams Fulfilled: The Pluralism of Religious Ends," 14.

specific interpretations. They contribute to the categories of religious experience in unique ways. According to Heim, "[i]f different religious practices and beliefs aim at and constitute distinct conditions of human fulfillment, then a very high proportion of what each tradition affirms may be true and valid in very much the terms that the tradition claims. This may be so even if deep conflict remains between the religions regarding priorities, background beliefs and ultimate metaphysical reality."[140]

Other scholars have made similar arguments, aligned with coherence-based theories of truth that recognize validity based on the ways that the propositions and practices of a lifestance cohere into a unified system. In Panikkar's framing, religions present different puzzles and thus different solutions, with an incommensurability of systems that is unbridgeable. Wilfred Cantwell Smith maintained that divine reality becomes manifest in the lives of individuals and communities through their religious traditions and can thus be understood as channels of divine revelation – necessarily plural. And Suchocki echoes that each path truly names God, offering the image of light: "Wave and particle are both truly light, and we live in a radically incarnational world where truth itself is a many-splendored thing."[141]

Some would argue that we should abandon truth as the lynchpin of value. Flemish philosopher Herman De Dijn asserts that religion is not really about truth in any event. Truth is a cognitive-scientific quest. Religion is about meaning, about being immersed in a particular and contingent tradition, belonging within a particular community. "Meaning is not about universal and objectifiable truth, but about 'truth-to-live-by,' unassailable and unmasterable."[142]

No logic of parity will be satisfactory to everyone. The value in this summary is cumulative, demonstrating the creative possibilities that undergird parity pluralism within monotheism.

4 Critiques of Parity Pluralism

There are a number of contemporary critiques leveled at pluralist frameworks. Some are theological, coming from more traditional or orthodox perspectives. One argument, for example, asserts that pluralists distort traditions to yield values that align with modernity. Another focuses on truth claims, maintaining that pluralism equals relativism and that the logic is unsustainable. A compelling critique, articulated in both emic and etic analyses, is that pluralism tends to universalize Western values and establish itself as the most highly

---

[140] Heim, "Dreams Fulfilled," 14.   [141] Suchocki, *Divinity and Diversity*, p. 52.
[142] Lieven Boeve, "The Particularity of Religious Truth Claims," in Helmer and De Troyer, *Truth*, pp. 185–186.

evolved position – thus undermining its pluralist claims. Looking at the modern study of religion, scholars also note that pluralist perspectives still ignore ways in which boundaries are permeable and fail to describe the complexity of religious difference. The theologies of religion on which they rely often limit what gets counted as religion and tend to privilege Christian or theist concerns. A number of these issues are raised, not only by opponents of parity pluralism, but also by pluralists who seek to improve the analytical strength of the discourse.

4.1 Distorts Traditions

Critiques take different forms depending on the underlying logic(s) of the pluralist argument. However, many contend that pluralists misread text and tradition. Adherents challenge Hick's identist pluralism, for example, arguing that their teachings cannot be reduced to metaphorical truths or metaphysical approximations. Ethical arguments for pluralism are contested for ignoring the spiritual hospitality possible in exclusivist and inclusivist perspectives. Presenting the Trinity as a capacious foundation for interreligious engagement, for instance, Rowan Williams writes: "The doctrines of Christian credal orthodoxy are not, as is regularly supposed, insuperable obstacles to dialogue; the incarnation of the logos is not the ultimate assertion of privilege and exclusivity."[143]

Challenges frequently focus on the selection and interpretation of texts. Contemporary Muslim theologian Yasir Qadhi writes that Qur'anic verses cited by pluralists are, in fact, (a) abrogated, (b) not teaching what the pluralists claim, or (c) applicable only before the coming of the Prophet Muhammad.[144] Timothy Winter, a neo-traditionalist Muslim scholar also known as Abdal Hakim Murad, argues that religious pluralism ignores the history of interpretation: "Religious pluralism, understood as the belief that the world religions represent a tapestry of differing but salvifically valid truth claims, is incompatible with Islamic monotheism." Citing the teaching of Ibn Qayyim al-Jawziyya (d. 1350) that "the ways to Hell are many, but the way to Heaven is one," Winter asserts that truth is disclosed through divine revelation – not constructed by human beings – and he provides a prooftext for Islamic supersession: "[He it is Who] sent His Messenger with guidance and the Religion of Truth to make it prevail over all religion" (9:33).[145]

---

[143] Rowan Williams, "Trinity and Pluralism," in D'Costa, *Christian Uniqueness Reconsidered*, p. 11.

[144] Qadhi, "The Path of Allah or the Paths of Allah?" in Khalil, *Between Heaven and Hell*, pp. 116–117.

[145] Winter, "Realism and the Real," in Khalil, *Between Heaven and Hell*, pp. 122, 125, 141.

Winter examines arguments from several pluralist Muslim thinkers, such as Farid Esack's understanding of a "believer" to include all believers in God. He counters that it disregards the historical Sunni consensus, as confirmed by al-Ghazali's (d. 1111) comment: "The Jews, Christians, and the followers of all the religions, whether Zoroastrians, idol-worshippers or others, are all to be considered unbelievers (*kafir*) as is specified in the Koran and agreed upon (*ijma*) by the Muslim community (*umma*)."[146]

Orthodox Jewish pluralists have also encountered challenges from within that claim their pluralist commitments misrepresent the tradition. When Jonathan Sacks, then the chief rabbi of the British Commonwealth, first published *The Dignity of Difference: How to Avoid the Clash of Civilizations* in 2002, two rabbinic critics insisted that his views were "irreconcilable with traditional Jewish teachings." A leading orthodox authority, Rabbi Yosef Shalom Elyashiv, agreed, so Sacks withdrew the edition and revised it. Explicit statements of parity, like "Judaism, Christianity, and Islam are religions of revelation – faiths in which God speaks and we attempt to listen," were removed, although Sacks' esteem for other traditions remained evident.[147]

Several Christian voices in *Four Views on Salvation in a Pluralistic World* (1995) contest John Hick's historical-critical, pluralist reading of scripture. Evangelical scholars R. Douglas Geivett and W. Gary Phillips, for example, assert that a more careful investigation into the Bible's textual difficulties would uncover rational explanations that do not "dilute the classical doctrine of biblical inerrancy." They identify Hick's distinction between the Jesus of history and the Christ of faith, and his claim that Jesus did not see himself as divine, as an erroneous reading of the biblical evidence.[148]

It is not uncommon for critics to cite verses to argue for the exclusivity of Christian truth, such as John 14:6: "I am the way and the truth and the life. No one comes to the Father except through me."[149] Pluralists are not unaware of such verses, of course, but they argue for different interpretations, understanding the exclusive language of scripture as confessional or love language rather than doctrine.[150] Krister Stendahl (1921–2008), for example, demonstrated the different interpretation that emerges if one examines the context. John 14 is part

---

[146] Winter, "The Last Trump Card: Islam and the Supersession of Other Faiths," p. 135.

[147] As recounted in Perry Schmidt-Leukel, *Religious Pluralism and Interreligious Theology*, chap. 3.

[148] Dennis L. Okholm and Timothy R. Phillips (eds.), *Four Views on Salvation in a Pluralistic World*, 71–76.

[149] See, for example, B. Reichert, "Why Is Religious Pluralism So Dangerous?" (May 30, 2023), www.christianity.com/wiki/cults-and-other-religions/why-is-religious-puralism-so-dangerous .html.

[150] See, for example, Knitter, *Introducing Theologies of Religion*, p. 133; Greenberg, *Living in the Image of God*, p. 79.

of Jesus' farewell conversation with the apostles, and they are tremendously fearful of what lies ahead. Jesus reassures them that there are many rooms in his Father's house, and that he is going ahead to prepare the way. His response is not a grand theological claim. Rather, it is an intimate reassurance that they will know the way to God because they have known Jesus, and they have already experienced the truth of this mystery.[151]

Pluralists are also aware that monotheistic traditions have historically been dominated by assumptions of superiority or supersession. While there are legitimate precedents for considering parity, pluralists recognize that they are innovating within tradition. Religious teachings have always been interpreted and reinterpreted in response to their historical contexts, however. Every reading of tradition is selective, shaped by its spiritual inheritance, the will of the interpreter, and the influence of one's time and place. A close reading of almost any religion demonstrates that it was not "born" as an unequivocally exclusive path. Parity pluralism is not a *mis*reading but a conscious rereading of monotheistic traditions, a recovery of the teachings that can serve as its foundation.

4.2 Promotes Relativism and Lacks Coherency

No single lifestance is more effective at transforming lives than another, and none is conclusively demonstrable in its claims. Yet the premise that diverse lifestances are of comparable merit has been attacked as relativism: How can teachings of ultimate value have no ultimate truth? Relativism holds that truth and value take shape in the context of specific cultures or worldviews; we cannot declare an objective standard.

"Relativism has been, in its various guises, both one of the most popular and most reviled philosophical doctrines of our time. Defenders see it as a harbinger of tolerance and the only ethical and epistemic stance worthy of the open-minded and tolerant. Detractors dismiss it for its alleged incoherence and uncritical intellectual permissiveness."[152] Those who deploy the term as an epithet often see relativism as postmodern capitulation to a culture in crisis after the collapse of Enlightenment ideals and historical positivism: Reason has revealed its limitations.[153] Relativism does not disavow reason in the way that opponents suggest, however, nor is it a new concept; the history of debate can be traced back to Plato.

Ironically, critiques of parity sometimes build on relativist assumptions to undercut ethically grounded pluralist arguments. How can we assess religious

---

[151] Stendahl, "From God's Perspective We Are All Minorities," 4.

[152] Baghramian and Carter, "Relativism."

[153] See, for example, Lesslie Newbigin, "Religion for the Marketplace," in D'Costa, *Christian Uniqueness Reconsidered*, 136–137.

paths by their capacity to shape moral action? If truth and falsity are contextually determined, then surely right and wrong are. For example, Akeel Bilgrami challenges Abou El Fadl's emphasis on justice as the criterion of religious value (and Muslim devotion) since the meanings of justice are multiple and contested.[154] Gavin D'Costa lifts up analyses by Stanley Hauerwas and Alasdair MacIntyre, contending that abstract values like justice cannot be separated from the tradition-specific narratives that determine their shape. "One religion's justice may be another's malpractice. ... [C]onsider the notion of justice in the abortion debate where it is regarded by some as just that a woman has a right over her own body in contrast to the view that it is just to protect the rights of the unborn foetus."[155] Whose justice designs the scorecard?

It is impossible to imagine, critics have argued, that one God of the universe would endorse contradictory teachings of truth and ethics. As Jewish philosopher Menachem Kellner writes:

> To my mind the "postmodern" approach takes an unfortunate reality – that we cannot agree on what is true, or even on what truth is – and turns it into an ideal. This position is, I think, self-refuting to the extent that it makes real communication among human beings impossible. It is also based upon a rejection of the idea of revelation, at least as it has been historically understood in Judaism, according to which the Torah is truth. This truth may be misunderstood; it may be viewed differently in different times; it may be better or worse understood as we get further from Sinai and closer to the Messiah; it may exist only in Heaven, here being approximated, but truth there is.[156]

He advocates monotheistic universalism in place of pluralism and relativism – not a triumph of Judaism, but a future in which all will come to know the one God and agree on God's truth. Interestingly, his allowance for the limited ways in which we may currently translate that truth echoes some parity pluralist arguments.

The assertion of parity is frequently faulted for a lack of coherence and rigor, violating the logical premise of noncontradiction. "This problem is already recognized by the *kalam* tradition," Tim Winter notes:

> In the twelfth century a theologian could respond to the claim that every religion must be true by observing that this would entail the concurrent validity of the belief in the created and the pre-eternal nature of the world, the existence

---

[154] Bilgrami, "The Importance of Democracy," in Cohen and Lague, *The Place of Tolerance in Islam*, p. 62. He was more persuaded that many Qur'anic instructions had to be interpreted in light of their historical context.

[155] D'Costa, "The Impossibility of a Pluralist View of Religions," 231.

[156] Kellner, "Overcoming Chosenness," 160.

and the nonexistence of the Creator God, monotheism and dualism, and the reality and the non-reality of the divine predicates – "and this is impossible."[157]

Pluralist frameworks address this logical challenge, even if critics are unpersuaded by the arguments. Convergent strategies suggest that diverse lifestances are each partial reflections of a singular transcendent reality. Pluralists who emphasize the limits of human understanding perceive religious truth claims as imperfect or incomplete. There are contradictions among religions because nobody has it quite right; faith in one's path can be embraced, but absolutism must be avoided. Monotheists who maintain that religious difference is divinely intended generally argue that God speaks to each society, even to each person, in ways that can cultivate meaning, purpose, and goodness in their lives; ultimate truth is not the object. Other pluralists maintain that truth itself is plural in ways that the logic of noncontradiction ignores.

Although some criticisms of parity may accidentally or deliberately misrepresent pluralist arguments, treating them as simplistic – and others may be blind to the logical inconsistencies in their own worldview – the press for intellectual rigor is a constructive dimension of the ongoing debate.

4.3 Universalizes Western Values with a New Exclusivism

The potential to universalize parity pluralism, as if it is a value-neutral theory of religion or the new "highest truth," presents an additional concern – it still establishes hierarchies among religious values and systems. Even the claim that parity pluralism is best positioned to foster interreligious understanding and advance the common good risks replacing religious absolutisms with a reinvented Western cultural imperialism that continues to impose its values on the world's religions. Consider that most of the publications and academic conferences promoting parity are based in North America and Europe, and it is no accident that the values align with the Enlightenment's emphasis on reason, unity, and egalitarianism.

Even with self-critical attention to the dynamics of power, it is potentially fraught to promote equality of religions without greater political, economic, and social equality among peoples and nations. The project may be blind to its own colonizing capacity. Catholic theologian Stephen J. Duffy points to a certain irony: "In a repentant post-colonial era, pluralist theory is willy-nilly implicated in a subtle intellectual supersessionism, a neo-colonialist form of discourse that constructs its other."[158] He contends that most theologies of religions operate on an a priori basis, making judgments about others based on one's own perspective; a posteriori analysis demands deep knowledge of other traditions and their

---

[157] Winter, "The Last Trump Card," 136, citing al-Nasafi.
[158] Duffy, "The Stranger within Our Gates," in Merrigan and Haers, *The Myriad Christ*, p. 13.

lived multiplicity, resisting the temptation to interpret those who orient around religion differently in our own terms. In the interim, he advocates for learned ignorance – not as a strategy for parity, but a rejection of religious absolutism.

Several pluralist thinkers, including S. Mark Heim, have also noted problems with constructing a metatheory of religion that claims to speak from above individual traditions. Parity pluralism is a socially contingent worldview; it must situate itself more resolutely within the discourse rather than over it.[159]

Other scholars have questioned whether parity pluralism is even possible. Paul Knitter suggests that perhaps we are all inclusivists. We cannot help but privilege our own worldview and interpret other lifestances through our own lens. Even if we recognize our perspective as a matter of personal preference rather than absolute value (as discussed in the section on ethics), we continuously process degrees of parity through our learning and encounters.[160] James Fredericks claims that Hicks' concept of the Real is a quasi-inclusivism that rests "on an assertion with no greater claim to veracity than any other conditioned statement of human belief."[161] Many pluralist strategies do mimic inclusivist postures: Diverse lifestances have value and their adherents can achieve ultimate spiritual purpose, but not on the basis that they imagine.

Gavin D'Costa argues that pluralism and inclusivism are, in fact, forms of exclusivism, and "nothing called pluralism really exists." They simply rely on different truth claims and criteria for assessing value. Analyzing Hick's philosophical pluralism, for example, D'Costa writes:

> [I]t is claimed that the Real cannot be known in itself and when any religion claims that the Real has revealed itself, then such claims are false. Such pluralism cannot tolerate alternative claims and is forced to deem them as mythical. The irony about tolerant pluralism is that it is eventually intolerant towards most forms of orthodox religious belief, Christian or otherwise."[162]

Individuals who affirm parity pluralism have, in fact, sometimes struggled to include those who see only their own lifestance as true or salvific among the "society of equals." In the world of interreligious engagement, Marion Larson and Sara Shady complain that theological exclusivists are frequently regarded as the problem to be discussed rather than persons with whom to interact, multiplying issues of misrecognition between exclusivists and pluralists.[163]

---

[159] Heim, *Salvations*, pp. 103–108.

[160] Knitter, *Introducing Theologies of Religions*, pp. 216–219.

[161] McCarthy, *Interfaith Encounters in America*, p. 30, summarizing Fredericks, *Faith Among Faiths: Christian Theology and Non-Christian Religions*.

[162] D'Costa, "Impossibility of a Pluralist View," 225, 229.

[163] Larson and Shady, "The Possibility of Solidarity," in Patel, Peace, and Silverman, *Interreligious/Interfaith Studies*, p. 154.

While excluding exclusivists negates claims of parity, including them might appear paradoxical. Yet almost all of the foundational logics of parity can make room for it. Epistemic humility suggests that we may all have something right, even if it is not the whole truth. Process thought sees God in relationship with *each* community in ways that can transform their lives – and for some that may be through faith in a singular supreme religion. Presumptions of our coformation press us to consider how certainty and ambiguity, boundaries and inclusiveness, illuminate each other.

Yet it is important to consider whether parity pluralism can or should include every lifestance. One seemingly straightforward criterion is to set those who advocate violence or coercion outside the bounds. Such an approach would echo pluralists who emphasize ethical criteria. As D'Costa notes about abortion, however, many forms of harm are disputed. Some might see gender equity as fundamental, thus excluding lifestances that advocate differentiated rights and roles or that insist on gender binaries. Others may question including a lifestance that affirms LGBTQ+ equality – or one that does not. Those with contrary opinions are not excluded from the interfaith "table," but moral nonnegotiables can limit convictions of parity. Can the frameworks of parity withstand ethical as well as theological differences?

4.4 Fails to Account for Complexity of Religious Difference

As mentioned in Section 3.4, identist strategies are criticized for failing to grapple adequately with the complexity of religious difference. In reinterpreting truth claims to reflect diverse impressions of "the Real," they are seen to reduce traditions to their commonalities (thus "reductive" pluralism) – erasing substantive differences or denying their significance. Hick, a common target of these critiques, has actually highlighted the plethora of differences as an argument for parity. Given the extraordinary multiplicity that exists *within* a single religion, he argued, we cannot assess any lifestance as a totality: "Each of these long traditions is so internally diverse, containing so many different kinds of both good and evil, that it is impossible for human judgement to weigh up and compare their merits as systems of salvation."[164]

Nonetheless, in trying to establish the grounds of parity, there is a tendency to essentialize religions. Discussions may ignore the disparity between text and the fluid, multifarious reality of lived tradition. Reified analysis, especially, fails to capture women's experiences.[165]

---

[164] Hick, *Problems of Religious Pluralism*, p. 86. For discussion of reductive pluralism, see Muhammad Legenhausen, "Nonreductive Pluralism and Religious Dialogue," in Khalil, *Between Heaven and Hell*, 153–158.

[165] See, for example, King, "Feminism," 40–55.

Some discussions have tried to reckon with the complexity of religious difference by refining the exclusivist–inclusivist–pluralist paradigm. Jacques Dupuis (1923–2004) identified Christian exclusivism as ecclesio-centrism, inclusivism as christocentrism, and pluralism as theocentrism. He argued that there is also logocentrism and pneumacentrism. Paul Knitter offers a fourfold paradigm with replacement, fulfilment, mutuality, and acceptance models. The last of these, which he subtitles "Many True Religions: So Be It," questions the need and ability to explain the existence of other religions. Episcopal theologian Drew Collins resurrects the typology of Hans Frei, seeking a generous orthodoxy that changes the questions altogether.[166]

Theologies of religion often still privilege Christian concerns and conceptual structures, since Christians are the most prolific producers of the discourse. Scholars may establish parity that works only for traditions that are theistic and scriptural or neglect lifestances that have not been part of the "world religions" paradigm. This has implications for nonreligious perspectives as well as neo-Pagans, Indigenous traditions, interspiritual identities, and others. As Janet Jakobsen notes, pluralism

> often presumes clearly delineated "units" of religious difference, most often located in well-recognized institutions of religious tradition with identifiable authorities who speak for the members of said tradition. Thus the model of pluralism can fail to recognize both diversity within religious traditions and forms of religious difference that do not fit this model of organization, for example, those that are not organized around authorities who can act as spokespersons, that are not institutionalized in recognizable (and hierarchical) structures, and that are delineated by practice or land rather than by beliefs about which one might speak.[167]

When such lifestances do get included in discussions of religious difference, the demand for intelligibility according to familiar standards can be just as problematic as neglect.[168]

John Cobb suggests that the problem is deeper: The very assumption that there is a defining essence that makes something a religion is faulty. After making a plausible argument that communism could be considered a religion, he declares, "There is no such thing as religion. There are only traditions,

---

[166] Dupuis, "Trinitarian Christology," in Merrigan and Haers, *The Myriad Christ*, p. 83; Knitter, *Introducing Theologies of Religions*; Collins, *The Unique and Universal Christ*.

[167] Jakobsen, "Ethics after Pluralism," in Bender and Klassen, *After Pluralism: Reimagining Religious Engagement*, p. 32.

[168] See, for example, Tracy Leavelle, "The Perils of Pluralism," in Bender and Klassen, *After Pluralism*, 156–177.

movements, communities, people, beliefs, and practices that have features that are associated by many people with what they mean by religion."[169]

There are analyses of religious difference that emphasize particularities: Instead of fitting religious others into one's own religious framework, "it is suggested that the truly ethical approach is to see them in terms of absolute alterity." Yet this discourse can effectively silence the conversation. "By insisting upon radical difference there can be no legitimate criticism from the Other towards your own tradition"[170] – and there may be nothing to talk about at all.

The complexity of religious difference must be seen intersectionally. Philosophical or theological hospitality may accompany cultural exclusion, for example. Bias is generally grounded in race, ethnicity, caste, or class more than theology, and arguments for parity often overlook these complicating dynamics. In addition, analyses too frequently presume clear boundaries and autonomous traditions when closer examination reveals how boundaries are permeable: "The notion of sealed traditions that underlies the language of pluralism and of clashing civilizations diverts our attention from the ways in which many traditions are mutually constitutive."[171]

Scholars who toil in the field of religious pluralism participate in these critiques. Mark Heim, for example, has problematized how theologies of religion too often yield monolithic treatment of "traditions" and monochromatic treatment of adherents. They also treat other lifestances in terms of their own confession, which cannot help but distort and imperialistically construct the "other," and they presume to define things that are beyond our capacity to discern. Still, he identifies the project as necessary. We all have beliefs about religious difference, whether we talk about them or not; theologies of religion require critical reflection and make us accountable to one another regarding our convictions. They provide an impetus for interreligious learning and a "docking mechanism" for what is learned, so it may find a place in the ongoing life and wisdom of one's own lifestance. They establish a discourse for those who stand between multiple traditions. And, in diverse societies, they can contribute to constructive relationships and moving past religious conflict.[172]

In short, the challenges do not undermine the foundations of parity, but they frame important questions for its ongoing self-critical development. Those that

---

[169] Cobb, "Beyond 'Pluralism,'" in D'Costa, *Christian Uniqueness Reconsidered*, p. 83.

[170] Paul Hedges, "Hospitality, Power and the Theology of Religions," 116–117.

[171] Amira Mittermeier, "A Matter of Interpretation: Dreams, Islam, and Psychology in Egypt," in Bender and Klassen, *After Pluralism*, p. 192.

[172] Heim, "The Shifting Significance of Theologies of Religious Pluralism," in Phan and Ray, *Understanding Religious Pluralism: Perspectives from Religious Studies and Theology*, chap. 16.

are most productive recognize the broad range of logics that, in fact, yield multiple religious pluralisms.

5 Concluding Remarks

One can be a religious pluralist without affirming parity among diverse life-stances. As discussed in Section 1, pluralism can simply denote the energetic engagement with diversity, actively seeking understanding across lines of difference.

In the process of authentic encounter, we nurture relationships of mutual respect and appreciation and advance the common good. It happens through sharing wisdom, generating creativity, and strengthening our capacity to live as good neighbors. Some efforts go further, undertaking additional acts of world repair. We also come to know ourselves more fully as we explain ourselves to others, see our lifestance through their eyes, and recognize how their worldview illuminates our own in fresh ways.

Practically, pluralists recognize that religious understanding is necessary to prevent human beings from killing or harming each other based on variances in belief or practice – a tragedy that is not confined to monotheistic religions. In the words of Abdulaziz Sachedina:

> The invocation of pluralism has become as much a summons as a celebration, an urgent exhortation to the citizens of the world to come to terms with their dizzying diversity. The endless conflicts between Christians and Muslims, Hindus and Sikhs, Tamils and Buddhists, and the attendant atrocities committed against innocent civilians, have imparted a direct urgency to the moral imperative of recognizing the human dignity of the other, regardless of his or her religious, ethnic, and cultural affiliations.[173]

Some scholars of religion focus on this broader understanding of pluralism because they see theologies of religion as a problematic exercise. There is an unavoidable distortion that occurs when we process other lifestances through our own theological or philosophical lens or try to synthesize wildly different and ever-changing traditions into a single analytical paradigm.

In addition, processes of definition are bound up with power. As William Scott Green notes: "A society does not simply discover its others, it fabricates them by selecting, isolating and emphasizing an aspect of another people's life and making it stand for their difference."[174] Religiously dominant voices define the terms of goodness, truth, and the essential dimensions of "faith," while determining what aspects of other lifestances matter and how to assess them.

---

[173] Sachedina, *Islamic Roots of Democratic Pluralism*, p. 22.
[174] Green, "Otherness Within," 50–51. See Edward Said, *Orientalism*, p. 332.

Even when trying to separate definitions from the assertion of dominance, their power looms large. Such concerns prompt efforts to engage positively with and understand religious "others" without trying to explain their existence.

It is also a fact that for many people – scholars, religious leaders, and adherents – parity pluralism is a bridge too far. They cannot affirm the sufficiency of religious traditions other than their own or find a logic to make space for competing truths. Yet a significant percentage still believe in the value of cultivating mutual understanding, moving beyond a tolerance that simply allows for each other's waywardness.

Pluralism, even without a conviction of parity, requires that we privilege building human relationships. We must see religious others in their full humanity and respect their freedoms. While we need not compromise our truth claims or worldview, and we can share the passion that roots our spiritual lives, the goal of meeting one another is not to make our own perspective prevail. With hospitality, humility, and empathy, we seek to understand the experience of people who orient around religion differently – and to value their contributions to the collective experience of humanity.

Parity pluralism can accomplish these goals, but it does not do so unfailingly. Communication Studies professors Charles Soukup and James Keaten illustrate how people can respond to religious otherness in humanizing or dehumanizing ways, regardless of their philosophical or theological convictions. They characterize humanizing responses as those that foster reciprocity, mutuality, self-reflexivity, authenticity, and compassion. Dehumanizing encounters sow fear, misrecognition, objectification, defensiveness, and a desire for control.[175] Theological exclusivists may recognize, for example, when their perspective makes others uncomfortable, and go out of their way to demonstrate respect for someone who believes differently. Parity pluralists may believe that everyone should embrace their point of view, demonstrating a desire for control, and they may misrecognize theological exclusivists as morally deficient.

One can readily muster support for pluralism as a humanizing encounter in monotheistic traditions. While not univocal, it appears to be less controversial than parity. Principles like hospitality, empathy, and the value of relationships are embedded in scriptural canons:

- "You shall not oppress a stranger, for you know the feelings of a stranger having yourselves been strangers in the land of Egypt" (Exod 23:9).
- "Do not neglect to show hospitality to strangers, for by doing that, some have entertained angels without knowing it" (Heb 13:2).

---

[175] Soukup and Keaten, "Humanizing and Dehumanizing Responses across Four Orientations to Religious Otherness," in Brown, *A Communication Perspective on Interfaith Dialogue*, 45–58.

- "Humanity! We created you from a male and a female, and made you into peoples and tribes so that you may come to know each other. The noblest among you in Allah's sight is the one with the most taqwa [God-consciousness]" (Qur'an 49:13).

In modern times, there have been official religious statements invoking this broader pluralism. The Second Vatican Council, for example, issued *Nostra aetate* in 1965, a paradigm-shattering statement of kinship with diverse religionists. While clearly not affirming parity, it acknowledges that Jews of today cannot be blamed for the death of Christ and that God is still in a covenantal relationship with them – for God's gifts and call are irrevocable (Rom 11:29). Islam, too, is dignified in the document by the manifold ways in which Muslims share Christian values.[176] Institutional investment by the Catholic Church substantially advanced projects of interreligious dialogue and related efforts, with several Protestant denominational bodies following suit.

Jewish communities around the world similarly engaged in this work. While there is no centralized religious authority comparable to the Vatican, 170 Jewish leaders across multiple denominations published a statement in 2000 (*Dabru Emet*) to recognize this new chapter in Jewish-Christian relations and to confirm key themes in mutual understanding.[177] In 2006, thirty-eight Islamic scholars from around the world issued "A Common Word," responding to Pope Benedict XVI's controversial Regensburg address by highlighting the shared emphasis on love of God and neighbor in Muslim and Christian traditions.[178] Both of these statements became productive platforms for interfaith conversation; they also sparked intrafaith discourse, as more people signed on and others disputed their claims.

Contemporary religious voices have grounded the work of pluralism in their individual lifestances, carefully incorporating key concerns that they do not want swallowed in pursuit of harmony. At the 2006 World Council of Churches gathering, for example, Rowan Williams (then Archbishop of Canterbury) declared:

> To work patiently alongside people of other faiths is not an option invented by modern liberals who seek to relativize the radical singleness of Jesus Christ and what was made possible through him. It is a necessary part of being where he is; it is a dimension of "liturgy", staying with the presence of God and the presence of God's creation (human and non-human) in prayer and love. If we are truly

---

[176] *Nostra aetate* (October 28, 1965): 1, www.vatican.va/archive/hist_councils/ii_vatican_council/documents/vat-ii_decl_19651028_nostra-aetate_en.html.

[177] "Dabru Emet: A Jewish Statement on Christians and Christianity" (September 10, 2000), https://icjs.org/dabru-emet-text/.

[178] "A Common Word," www.acommonword.com/the-acw-document/.

learning how to be in that relation with God and the world in which Jesus of Nazareth stood, we shall not turn away from those who see from another place.[179]

In similar fashion, Jeremy Kalmanofsky, a leading rabbi in the Conservative movement, affirms the importance of engagement as a Jewish value while simultaneously protecting particularity:

> Contemporary Conservative Jews must seek a dialectical balance with the adherents of other religions, becoming partners with them to work for the common weal, while also striving to maintain the boundaries that define our Jewish identity. . . . Though religious and social barriers separate us from non-Jews in some way, ethical obligations still bind us all together as human beings created in God's image.[180]

Muhammad Shafiq and Mohammed Abu-Nimer draw from Islam's long history of engagement with diverse religious communities to make a case to the contemporary English-speaking Muslim community that actively seeking understanding across religious differences is an authorized activity.[181]

The current volume need not build a case for pluralism of this sort; there are numerous books to which one might refer for such a discussion.[182] It is worth highlighting, however, that the challenge of truly pluralistic engagement is substantial even without parity. Every scholarly effort and project in the field tries to discern how to do it well. In excavating space for parity without denying that there are other ways to read the traditions, this Element hopes to contribute to the pluralist project.

---

[179] Williams, "Christian Identity and Religious Plurality."

[180] Kalmanofsky, "Interfaith Relations," in Cohen, *The Observant Life*, p. 728.

[181] Shafiq and Abu-Nimer, *Interfaith Dialogue: A Guide for Muslims*.

[182] See, for example, Boys and Lee, *Christians and Jews in Dialogue*; Cornille, *The Im-Possibility of Interreligious Dialogue*; Grundmann (ed.), *Interreligious Dialogue*; Shafiq and Abu-Nimer, *Interfaith Dialogue*; Swidler, Duran, and Firestone, *Trialogue*.

Bibliography

Aijaz, Imran. "Traditional Islamic Exclusivism: A Critique." *European Journal for the Philosophy of Religion* 6, no. 2 (Summer 2014): 185–209.

Al-Azami, Muhammad Mustafa. *The History of the Qur'ānic Text: From Revelation to Compilation*. London: UK Islamic Academy, 2002. www.kalamullah.com/Books/history_of_quranic_text.pdf.

Al-Fayyumi, Natan'el. *Bustan al-Ukul*. Translated and edited by David Levine. Piscataway: Gorgias Press, 2009.

Ali, Kecia and Oliver Leaman. *Islam: The Key Concepts*. New York: Routledge, 2008. https://doi.org/10.4324/9780203934234.

Amaladoss, Michael. *Interreligious Encounters: Opportunities and Challenges*. Edited by Jonathan Y. Tan. Maryknoll: Orbis Books, 2017.

Arkoun, Mohammed. *The Unthought in Contemporary Islamic Thought*. London: Saqi Books, 2002.

Asani, Ali S. "So You May Know One Another: A Muslim American Reflects on Pluralism and Islam." *The Annals of the American Academy of Political and Social Science* 588, no. 1 (July 2003): 40–51. https://doi.org/10.1177/0002716203588001004.

Askari, Hasan. "Within and Beyond the Experience of Religious Diversity." In *The Experience of Religious Diversity*, edited by John Hick and Hasan Askari, 191–218. Aldershot: Gower, 1985.

Augustine of Hippo. *Confessions*. Translated by R. S. Pine-Coffin. New York: Penguin, 1961.

Aydin, Mahmout. "Islam in a World of Diverse Faiths – A Muslim View." In *Islam and Inter-Faith Relations*, edited by Lloyd Ridgeon and Perry Schmidt-Leukel, 33–54. London: SCM Press, 2007.

Ayoub, Mahmoud. "Islam and the Challenge of Religious Pluralism." *Global Dialogue* 2 (2000): 55–58.

"Nearest in Amity: Christians in the Qur'an and Contemporary Exegetical Tradition." *Islam and Christian-Muslim Relations* 8, no. 2 (1997): 145–164. https://doi.org/10.1080/09596419708721117.

Bachya ibn Pakuda. *Duties of the Heart* (Chovot haLevavot). Translated by Yaakov Feldman. Lanham: Jason Aronson, 1996.

Baghramian, Maria and J. Adam Carter. "Relativism." In *The Stanford Encyclopedia of Philosophy*, edited by Edward N. Zalta. Stanford: Stanford University Metaphysics Research Lab. Spring 2022 ed. https://plato.stanford.edu/archives/spr2022/entries/relativism/.

Barnes, Michael. *Interreligious Learning: Dialogue, Spirituality, and the Christian Imagination*. Cambridge: Cambridge University Press, 2011. https://doi.org/10.1017/CBO9781139003285.

Barton, John. *Better Religion: A Primer for Interreligious Peacebuilding*. Waco: Baylor University Press, 2022.

Bauer, Walter. *Orthodoxy and Heresy in Earliest Christianity*. Minneapolis: Fortress Press, 1979.

Bauman, Zygmunt. *Modernity and Ambivalence*. Cambridge: Polity Press, 1993.

Bender, Courtney and Pamela E. Klassen, eds. *After Pluralism*: *Reimagining Religious Engagement*. New York: Columbia University Press, 2010.

Benin, Stephen D. *Footprints of God: Divine Accommodation in Jewish and Christian Thought*. Albany: State University of New York Press, 1993. http://doi.org/10.1353/book10447.

Berkowitz, Beth. *Defining Jewish Difference*. Cambridge: Cambridge University Press, 2012. https://doi.org/10.1017/CBO9781139005159.

Berman, Saul. "*Lifnim Mishurat Hadin*." *Journal of Jewish Studies* 26, no. 1 (1975): 86–104; 28, no. 2 (1977): 181–193. https://doi.org/10.18647/740/JJS-1975.

Bidwell, Duane R. *When One Religion Isn't Enough: The Lives of Spiritually Fluid People*. Boston: Beacon Press, 2018.

Boase, Roger, ed. *Islam and Global Dialogue: Religious Pluralism and the Pursuit of Peace*. London: Routledge, 2005. https://doi.org/10.4324/9781315589909.

Bock, Jan-Jonathan, John Fahy, and Samuel Everett, eds. *Emergent Religious Pluralisms*. Cham: Palgrave MacMillan, 2019. https://doi.org/10.1007/978-3-030-13811-0.

Boulouque, Clémence. *Another Modernity: Elia Benamozegh's Jewish Universalism*. Stanford: Stanford University Press, 2020.

Boys, Mary C., and Sarah S. Lee. *Christians and Jews in Dialogue: Learning in the Presence of the Other*. Woodstock: SkyLight Paths, 2006.

Brill, Alan. *Judaism and Other Religions: Models of Understanding*. New York: Palgrave Macmillan, 2010. https://doi.org/10.1057/9780230105683.

Brock, Rita Nakashima and Rebecca Ann Parker. *Saving Paradise: How Christianity Traded Love of This World for Crucifixion and Empire*. Boston: Beacon Press, 2008.

Brown, Jonathan A. C. *Misquoting Muhammad: The Challenges and Choices of Interpreting the Prophet's Legacy*. London: OneWorld, 2015.

Buber, Martin. *I and Thou*. Translated by Walter Kaufmann. Edinburgh: T. & T. Clark, 1970.

Burrell, David B. "Anthropomorphism in Catholic Contexts." In *Whose God? Which Tradition?*, edited by Dewi Z. Phillips, 129–136. New York: Ashgate, 2021. https://doi.org/10.4324/9781315234090.

Casarella, Peter. *Cusanus: The Legacy of Learned Ignorance.* Washington:Catholic University of America Press, 2006. https://doi.org/10.2307/j.ctt284vvk.

Cascante-Gómez, Fernando A. "Latin American Theology and Religious Pluralism: A Latin American Voice." *Religious Education* 104, no. 5 (2009): 556–563. https://doi.org/10.1080/00344080903294012.

Chandhoke, Neera. *Rethinking Pluralism, Secularism and Tolerance: Anxieties of Coexistence.* New Delhi: SAGE, 2019.

Chazan, Robert. *The Jews of Medieval Western Christendom 1000–1500.* Cambridge: Cambridge University Press, 2006. https://doi.org/10.1017/CBO9780511818325.

Cheetham, David, Douglas Pratt, and David, Thomas, eds. *Understanding Interreligious Relations.* Oxford: Oxford University Press, 2013.

Chittick, William. *Imaginal Worlds: Ibn al-'Arabi and the Problem of Religious Diversity.* Albany: State University of New York Press, 1994.

Clooney, Francis X. *Comparative Theology: Deep Learning across Religious Borders.* Hoboken: Wiley, 2010.

Learning Interreligiously: In the Text, In the World. Minneapolis: Augsburg Fortress, 2018.

Cobb, John B., Jr. *Beyond Dialogue: Toward a Mutual Transformation of Christianity and Buddhism.* Eugene: Wipf & Stock, 1998.

Cohen, Charles L. and Ronald L. Numbers, eds. *Gods in America: Religious Pluralism in the United States.* New York: Oxford University Press, 2013. https://doi.org/10.1093/acprof:oso/9780199931903.001.0001.

Cohen, Joshua and Ian Lague, eds. *The Place of Tolerance in Islam: Khaled Abou El Fadl with Taiq Ali, Milton Viorst, John Esposito, and Others.* Boston: Beacon Press, 2002.

Cohen, Mark R., Sydney H. Griffith, Hava Lazarus-Yafeh, and Sasson Somekh, eds. *The Majlis: Interreligious Encounters in Medieval Islam.* Weisbaden: Harrassowitz, 1999.

Cohn-Sherbok, Dan. *Judaism and Other Faiths.* New York: St. Martin's Press, 1994.

Collins, Drew. *The Unique and Universal Christ: Refiguring the Theology of Religions.* Waco: Baylor University Press, 2021.

Cornille, Catherine. *The Im-Possibility of Interreligious Dialogue.* New York: Crossroad, 2008.

Cornille, Catherine, ed. *The Wiley-Blackwell Companion to Inter-Religious Dialogue.* Chichester: John Wiley & Sons, 2013. https://doi.org/10.1002/9781118529911.

D'Costa, Gavin. "The Impossibility of a Pluralist View of Religions." *Religious Studies* 32 (January 1996): 223–232. https://doi.org/10.1017/S0034412500 024240.

    Vatican II: Catholic Doctrines on Jews and Muslims. New York: Oxford University Press, 2014. https://doi.org/10.1093/acprof:oso/9780199659272 .001.0001.

D'Costa, Gavin, ed. *Christian Uniqueness Reconsidered: The Myth of a Pluralistic Theology of Religions*. Maryknoll: Orbis Books, 1990.

Depoortere, Frederiek, and Magdalen Lambkin, eds. *The Question of Theological Truth: Philosophical and Interreligious Perspectives*. Amsterdam: Rodopi, 2012.

Eck, Diana L. *Encountering God: A Spiritual Journey from Bozeman to Banaras*. Boston: Beacon Press, 2003.

    A New Religious America: How a "Christian Country" Became the World's Most Religiously Diverse Nation. New York: HarperCollins, 2002.

    "Pluralism: Problems and Promise." *Journal of Interreligious Studies* 17 (2015). https://irstudies.org/index.php/jirs/article/view/309/287.

    "Prospects for Pluralism: Voice and Vision in the Study of Religion." *Journal of the American Academy of Religion* 75, no. 4 (2007): 743–776. https://doi.org/10.1093/jaarel/lfm061.

Ellethy, Yaser. *Islam, Context, Pluralism and Democracy: Classical and Modern Interpretations*. London: Routledge, 2014. https://doi.org/10.4324/97813 15755533.

El Shamsy, Ahmed. "The Social Construction of Orthodoxy." In *The Cambridge Companion to Classical Islamic Theology*, edited by Tim Winter, 97–120. Cambridge: Cambridge University Press, 2008. https://doi.org/10.1017/ CCOL9780521780582.006.

Esack, Farid. "Muslims Engaging the Other and the Humanum." *Emory University International Law Review* 14, no. 2 (2000): 529–569.

    Quran, Liberation and Pluralism: An Islamic Perspective of Interreligious Solidarity Against Oppression. London: OneWorld, 1996.

Esposito, John, ed. *The Oxford History of Islam*. Oxford: Oxford University Press, 1999. https://doi.org/10.1093/acref/9780195107999.001.0001.

Essa, Ahmed. *Studies in Islamic Civilization: The Muslim Contribution to the Renaissance*. Herndon: International Institute of Islamic Thought, 2012.

Etherington, Norman ed. *Missions and Empire*. Oxford: Oxford University Press, 2005. https://doi.org/10.1093/acprof:oso/9780199253487.001 .0001.

Eusebius. *Ecclesiastical History*. Translated by Arthur Cushman McGiffert. New York: Christian Literature, 1890.

Falk, Harvey. "Rabbi Jacob Emden's Views on Christianity." *Journal of Ecumenical Studies* 19, no. 1 (Winter 1982): 105–111.

Fatoohi, Looay. *Abrogation in the Qur'an and Islamic Law.* London: Routledge, 2012. https://doi.org/10.4324/9780203096208.

Fernandez, Eleazar S., ed. *Teaching for a Multifaith World.* Eugene: Wipf & Stock, 2017.

Fernández-Morera, Darío. *The Myth of the Andalusian Paradise: Muslims, Christians and Jews under Islamic Rule in Medieval Spain.* Wilmington: Intercollegiate Studies Institute, 2016.

Fletcher, Jeannine Hill. *Monopoly on Salvation? A Feminist Approach to Religious Pluralism.* New York: Continuum, 2005. https://doi.org/10.5040/9781472549938.

"Shifting Identity: The Contribution of Feminist Thought to Theologies of Religious Pluralism." *Journal of Feminist Studies in Religion* 19 (2003): 5–24.

Foucault, Michel. *Power/Knowledge: Selected Interview and Other Writings, 1972–1977.* New York: Pantheon Books, 1980.

Fredrickson, George. *Racism: A Short History.* Princeton: Princeton University Press, 2002.

Funkenstein, Amos. *Perceptions of Jewish History.* Berkeley: University of California Press, 1993.

Gamble, Harry. *The New Testament Canon: Its Making and Meaning.* Eugene: Wipf and Stock, 2002.

Gimaret, Daniel, and Guy Monnot, trans. *Livre des Religions et des Sectes.* Leuven: Peeters/Unesco, 1986.

Giordan, Guiseppe and Andrew Lynch, eds. *Interreligious Dialogue: From Religion to Geopolitics.* Leiden: Brill, 2019. https://doi.org/10.1163/9789004401266.

Goddard, Hugh. *A History of Christian–Muslim Relations.* Chicago: New Amsterdam Books, 2000.

Goshen-Gottstein, Alon. *The Religious Other: Hostility, Hospitality, and the Hope of Human Flourishing.* Eugene: Wipf & Stock, 2018.

Goshen-Gottstein, Alon, ed. *Religious Truth: Towards a Jewish Theology of Religions.* Littman Library of Jewish Civilization. London: Liverpool University Press, 2020.

Goshen-Gottstein, Alon and Eugene Korn, eds. *Jewish Theology and World Religions.* Portland: Littman Library of Jewish Civilization, 2012.

Graham, Daniel W. "Heraclitus (fl. C. 500 B.C.E.)." *Internet Encyclopedia of Philosophy.* https://iep.utm.edu/heraclit/.

Green, William Scott. "Otherness Within: Towards a Theory of Difference in Rabbinic Judaism." In *To See Ourselves as Others See Us: Christians, Jews, "Others" in Late Antiquity*, edited by Jacob Neusner and Ernest S. Frerichs, 49–69. Chico: Scholar Press, 1985.

Greenberg, Irving. *For the Sake of Heaven and Earth: The New Encounter Between Judaism and Christianity*. Philadelphia: Jewish Publication Society, 2004.

Living in the Image of God. Lanham: Jason Aronson, 1998.

Griffin, David Ray, ed. *Deep Religious Pluralism*. Louisville: Westminster John Knox, 2005.

Grundmann, Christoffer H., ed. *Interreligious Dialogue: An Anthology of Voices Bridging Cultural and Religious Divides*. Winona: Anselm Academic, 2015.

Grung, Anne Hege. "Interreligious Dialogue: Moving Between Compartmentalization and Complexity." *Approaching Religion* 1, no. 1 (May 2011): 26–32, https://doi.org/10.30664/ar.67467.

Gustafson, Hans. *Everyday Wisdom: Interreligious Studies in a Pluralistic World*. Minneapolis: Fortress Press, 2023.

Gustafson, Hans, ed. *Interreligious Studies: Dispatches from an Emerging Field*. Waco: Baylor University Press, 2020.

Learning from Other Religious Traditions: Leaving Room for Holy Envy. Pathways for Ecumenical and Interreligious Dialogue. New York: Palgrave Macmillan, 2018.

Gutierrez, Gustavo. " Hermeneutic of Hope." Occasional Paper No. 13, The Center for Latin American Studies, Vanderbilt University, 2012.

Halbertal, Moshe. "'Ones Possessed of Religion': Religious Tolerance in the Teachings of the Me'iri." *Edah* 1, no. 1 (2000): 1–24.

People of the Book: Canon, Meaning and Authority. Cambridge: Harvard University Press, 1997.

Hall, David, ed. *Lived Religion in America*. Princeton: Princeton University Press, 1997.

Harris, Elizabeth, Paul Hedges, and Shanthikumar Hettiarachchi, eds. *Twenty-First Century Theologies of Religion: Retrospection and Future Prospects*. Leiden: Brill, 2016. https://doi.org/10.1163/9789004324077.

Hartman, David. *Conflicting Visions: Spiritual Possibilities of Modern Israel*. New York: Schocken Books, 1990.

Hayes, Christine. "Legal Truth, Right Answers and Best Answers: Dworkin and the Rabbis." *Diné Yisrael* 25 (2008): 73–121.

"The 'Other' in Rabbinic Literature." In *The Cambridge Companion to the Talmud and Rabbinic Literature*, edited by Charlotte Fonrobert and

Martin Jaffee, 243–269. Cambridge: Cambridge University Press, 2007. https://doi.org/10.1017/CCOL0521843901.012.

What's Divine about Divine Law? Early Perspectives. Princeton: Princeton University Press, 2015.

Hedges, Paul. *Controversies in Interreligious Dialogue and the Theology of Religion*. London: SCM Press, 2010.

"Hospitality, Power and the Theology of Religions: Prophethood in the Abrahamic Context." In *Interreligious Engagement and Theological Reflection*, edited by Douglas Pratt, Angela Berlis, and Andreas Krebs, 112–135. Bern: Peter Lang, 2014.

Understanding Religions: Theories and Methods for Studying Religiously Diverse Societies. Berkeley: University of California Press, 2021.

Heft, James L., Reuven Firestone, and Omid Safi, eds. *Learned Ignorance: Intellectual Humility Among Jews, Christians, and Muslims*. Oxford: Oxford University Press, 2011. https://doi.org/10.1093/acprof:osobl/97801997693 08.001.0001.

Hegel, Georg. *Encyclopaedia of the Philosophical Sciences*. Translated and edited by Klaus Brinkmann and Daniel Dahlstrom. Cambridge: Cambridge University Press, 2010.

Heim, S. Mark. "Dreams Fulfilled: The Pluralism of Religious Ends." *Christian Century* 118, no. 2 (January 17, 2001): 14–19. www.christiancentury.org/article/dreams-fulfilled.

Salvations: Truth and Difference in Religion. Maryknoll: Orbis Books, 1995.

Helmer, Christine and Kristin De Troyer, eds. *Truth: Interdisciplinary Dialogues in a Pluralist Age*. Leuven: Peeters Publishers, 2003.

Heschel, Abraham Joshua. "No Religion Is an Island," *Union Seminary Quarterly Review* 21, no. 2 (1966): 117–134.

Hick, John. *God and the Universe of Faiths*. London: Macmillan, 1973.

An Interpretation of Religion: Human Responses to the Transcendent. 2nd ed. New Haven, CT: Yale University Press, 2005.

Problems of Religious Pluralism. New York: Springer, 1985.

Hick, John, and Paul Knitter, eds. *The Myth of Christian Uniqueness: Toward a Pluralistic Theology of Religions*. Eugene: Wipf & Stock, 2005.

Howard, Thomas Albert. *The Faiths of Others: A History of Interreligious Dialogue*. New Haven: Yale University Press, 2021.

Hume, David. *Dialogues and Natural History of Religion*. Oxford: Oxford University Press, 2009.

Hustwit, J. R. *Interreligious Hermeneutics and the Pursuit of Truth*. Lanham: Lexington Books, 2014.

Huxley, Aldous. *The Perennial Philosophy: An Interpretation of the Great Mystics, East and West*. New York: Harper and Brothers, 1945.

Ibn al'Arabi. *The Bezels of Wisdom*. Translated by R. W. J. Austin. Mahwah: Paulist Press, 1980.

    The Tarjuman al-Ashwaq. Translated by Reynold Nicholson. London: Royal Asiatic Society, 1911.

Imhof, Paul, and Hubert Biallowons, eds. *Karl Rahner in Dialogue: Conversations and Interviews, 1965–1982*. Translated by Harvey D. Egan. New York: Crossroad, 1986.

Isaac the Syrian. *The Wisdom of St. Isaac the Syrian*. Translated by Sebastian Brock. Oxford: SLG Press, 1997.

Kalmanofsky, Jeremy. "Interfaith Relations." In *The Observant Life: The Wisdom of Conservative Judaism for Contemporary Jews*, edited by Martin S. Cohen, 727–750. New York: The Rabbinical Assembly, 2012.

Kamali, Muhammad Hashim. *Principles of Islamic Jurisprudence*. Cambridge: Islamic Texts Society, 2005.

Kant, Immanuel. *Religion within the Boundaries of Mere Reason and Other Writings*. Translated by Allen Wood and George di Giovanni. Cambridge: Cambridge University Press, 1998. https://doi.org/10.1017/CBO978051 1809637.

Karabell, Zachary. *Peace Be Upon You: Fourteen Centuries of Muslim, Christian, and Jewish Conflict and Cooperation*. New York: Vintage Books, 2008.

Kaveny, Cathleen. *Prophecy without Contempt: Religious Discourse in the Public Square*. Cambridge, MA: Harvard University Press, 2016.

Keller, Catherine. *The Face of the Deep: A Theology of Becoming*. London: Routledge, 2002. https://doi.org/10.4324/9780203451731.

Kellner, Menachem. "Overcoming Chosenness." In *Covenant and Chosenness in Judaism and Mormonism*, edited by Raphael Jospe, Truman G. Madsen, and Seth Ward, 147–172. Madison: Farleigh Dickinson University Press, 2001.

Khalil, Mohammad Hassan, ed. *Between Heaven and Hell: Islam, Salvation, and the Fate of Others*. Oxford: Oxford University Press, 2013. https://doi .org/10.1093/acprof:oso/9780199945399.001.0001.

Kierkegaard, Søren. *Concluding Unscientific Postscript to "Philosophical Fragments."* Translated by Howard and Edna Hong. Princeton: Princeton University Press, 1992.

Kilp, A. "Religion in the Construction of the Cultural 'Self' and 'Other.'" *ENDC Proceedings* 14, no. 2 (2011): 197–222.

King, Richard *Orientalism and Religion: Postcolonial Theory, India, and "The Mystic East."* London: Routledge, 1999. https://doi.org/10.4324/9780203 006085.

King, Ursula. "Feminism: The Missing Dimension in the Dialogue of Religions." In *Pluralism and Religions: The Theological and Political Dimensions*, edited by John May, 40–55. London: Cassell Academic, 1998.

Knitter, Paul F. *Introducing Theologies of Religions*. Maryknoll: Orbis Books, 2012.

One Earth, Many Religions: Multifaith Dialogue and Global Responsibility. Maryknoll: Orbis Books, 1995.

Knitter, Paul F., ed. *The Myth of Religious Superiority: A Multifaith Exploration*. Maryknoll: Orbis Books, 2005.

Kolbrener, William. "Chiseled on All Sides: Hermeneutics and Dispute in Rabbinic Tradition." *AJS Review* 28, no. 2 (November 2004): 273–295. https://doi.org/10.1017/S0364009404000170.

Kraemer, David. *Mind of the Talmud: An Intellectual History of the Bavli*. New York: Oxford University Press, 1990.

Kurzman, Charles, ed. *Liberal Islam: A Sourcebook*. Oxford: Oxford University Press, 1998.

Lamptey (now Rhodes), Jerusha. *Never Wholly Other: A Muslima Theology of Religious Pluralism*. Oxford: Oxford University Press, 2014. https://doi .org/10.1093/acprof:oso/9780199362783.001.0001.

Landau, Yehezkel. "Interfaith Leadership Training at Hartford Seminary: The Impact of the Advanced 'Building Abrahamic Partnerships Course.'" DMin Thesis, Hartford Seminary, 2013.

Latief, Hilman. "Comparative Religion in Medieval Muslim Literature." *American Journal of Islamic Social Sciences* 23, no. 4 (2006): 28–62. https://doi.org/10.35632/ajis.v23i4.446.

Leirvik, Oddbjørn. *Interreligious Studies: A Relational Approach to Religious Activism and the Study of Religion*. New York: Bloomsbury, 2014. https:// doi.org/10.5040/9781472594655.

Machinist, Peter. "Once More: Monotheism in Biblical Israel." *Journal of the Interdisciplinary Study of Monotheistic Religions*, Special Issue (2006): 25–39.

Markofski, Wes. "Reflexive Evangelicalism." In *Religion, Humility, and Democracy in a Divided America*, edited by Ruth Braunstein, 47–74. Bingley: Emerald, 2019. https://doi.org/10.1108/S0198-8719201900 00036004.

Maimonides, Moses. *Mishneh Torah*. Translated by Eliyahu Touger. New York: Moznaim, 1998.

Masuzawa, Tomoko. *The Invention of World Religions: Or, How European Universalism Was Preserved in the Language of Pluralism*. Chicago: University of Chicago Press, 2005.

McCarthy, Kate. *Interfaith Encounters in America*. New Brunswick: Rutgers University Press, 2007.

McGraw, Barbara and Jo Renee Formicola, eds. *Taking Religious Pluralism Seriously: Spiritual Politics on America's Sacred Ground*. Waco: Baylor University Press, 2007.

McKim, Robert, ed. *Religious Perspectives on Religious Diversity*. Leiden: Brill, 2016. https://doi.org/10.1163/9789004330436.

Meddeb, Abdelwahab, and Benjamin Stora, eds. *A History of Jewish–Muslim Relations: From the Origins to the Present Day*. Translated by Jane Marie Todd and Michael B. Smith. Princeton: Princeton University Press, 2013.

Meir, Ephraim. *Interreligious Theology: Its Value and Mooring in Modern Jewish Philosophy*. Berlin: de Gruyter, 2015. https://doi.org/10.1515/978311 0430455.

Meister, Chad, ed. *The Oxford Handbook of Religious Diversity*. Oxford: Oxford University Press, 2010. https://doi.org/10.1093/oxfordhb/9780195 340136.001.0001.

Mendelssohn, Moses. *Jerusalem and Other Jewish Writings*. Translated and edited by Alfred Jospe. New York: Schocken Books, 1969.

"Letter to Johann Casper Lavater." In *Disputation and Dialogue: Readings in the Jewish-Christian Encounter*, edited by Frank Ephraim Talmage, 265–272. New York: KTAV, 1975.

Menocal, María Rosa. *The Ornament of the World: How Muslims, Jews and Christians Created a Culture of Tolerance in Medieval Spain*. New York: Back Bay Books, 2002.

Merrigan, Terrence and John Friday, eds. *The Past, Present, and Future of Theologies of Interreligious Dialogue*. London: Oxford University Press, 2017. https://doi.org/10.1093/acprof:oso/9780198792345.001.0001.

Merrigan, Terrence and J. Haers, eds. *The Myriad Christ: Plurality and the Quest for Unity in Contemporary Christology*. Leuven: Leuven University Press, 2000.

Mikva, Rachel S. *Dangerous Religious Ideas: The Deep Roots of Self-Critical Faith in Judaism, Christianity, and Islam*. Boston: Beacon Press, 2020.

Interreligious Studies: An Introduction. Cambridge: Cambridge University Press, 2023. https://doi.org/10.1017/9781108920056.

Min, Kyongsuk. "Dialectical Pluralism and Solidarity of Others—Towards a New Paradigm." *Journal of the American Academy of Religions* 65 (1997): 587–604. https://doi.org/10.1093/jaarel/65.3.587.

Moerdler, Zahava. "Racializing Antisemitism: The Development of Racist Antisemitism and Its Current Manifestations." *Fordham International Law Journal* 40, no. 4 (2017): 1281–1325.

Moosa, Ebrahim. "The Debts and Burdens of Critical Islam." In *Progressive Muslims: On Justice, Gender, and Pluralism*, edited by Omid Safi, 111–127. Oxford: OneWorld, 2003.

Mosher, Lucinda, ed. *The Georgetown Companion to Interreligious Studies*. Washington, DC: Georgetown University Press, 2022. https://doi.org/10.2307/j.ctv27qzsb3.

Mosher, Lucinda, Axel Marc Oaks Takacs, Or N. Rose, and Mary Elizabeth Moore, eds. *Deep Understanding for Divisive Times: Essays Marking a Decade of the Journal of Interreligious Studies*. Newton Centre: Interreligious Studies Press, 2020.

Moyaert, Marianne. *Fragile Identities: Towards a Theology of Interreligious Hospitality*. Amsterdam: Rodopi, 2011.

Nasr, Seyyed Hossein. *Knowledge and the Sacred*. Albany: SUNY Press, 1989.

Nasr, Seyyed Hossein, ed. *The Study Quran: A New Translation and Commentary*. New York: HarperOne, 2015.

Nicholas of Cusa. *Nicholas of Cusa on Interreligious Harmony: Text, Concordance and Translation of De Pace Fidei*. Edited and translated by James Biechler and H. Lawrence Bond. Lewiston: Edwin Mellen, 1991.

Niebuhr, Gustav. *Beyond Tolerance: Searching for Interfaith Understanding in America*. New York: Viking, 2008.

Norton, Michael Barnes. "Religious Pluralism." *Internet Encyclopedia of Philosophy*. https://iep.utm.edu/rel-plur/.

Nostra aetate. (October 28, 1965). www.vatican.va/archive/hist_councils/ii_vatican_council/documents/vat-ii_decl_19651028_nostra-aetate_en.html.

Okholm, Dennis L., and Timothy R. Phillips, eds. *Four Views on Salvation in a Pluralistic World*. Grand Rapids: Zondervan, 1995.

Olawoyin, Olusegun Noah. "Varieties of Religious Pluralism," *Journal of Arts and Humanities* 4, no. 12 (December 2015): 50–58. https://doi.org/10.18533/journal.v4i12.870.

Panikkar, Raimon. *A Dwelling Place for Wisdom*. Louisville: Westminster John Knox, 1993.

    Invisible Harmony: Essays on Contemplation and Responsibility. Minneapolis: Fortress Press, 1995.

Patel, Eboo. *Interfaith Leadership: A Primer*. Boston: Beacon Press, 2016.

Out of Many Faiths: Religious Diversity and the American Promise. Princeton: Princeton University Press, 2018.

Patel, Eboo, Jennifer Howe Peace, and Noah Silverman, eds. *Interreligious/ Interfaith Studies: Defining a New Field.* Boston: Beacon Press, 2018.

Patton, Laurie L. "Toward a Pragmatic Pluralism." *Emory Magazine* (Autumn 2006). www.emory.edu/EMORY_MAGAZINE/autumn2006/essay_plur alism.htm.

Peace, Jennifer Howe. "Coformation through Interreligious Learning." *Colloquy* 20, no. 1 (Fall 2011): 24–26.

Peace, Jennifer Howe, Or N. Rose, and Gregory Mobley, eds. *My Neighbor's Faith: Stories of Interreligious Encounter, Growth, and Transformation.* Maryknoll: Orbis Books, 2012.

Phan, Peter C. *Understanding Religious Pluralism: Perspectives from Religious Studies and Theology.* Eugene: Pickwick Publications, 2014.

Pines, Shlomo. "The Limitations of Human Knowledge According to Al-Farabi, ibn Bajja, and Maimonides." In *Studies in Medieval Jewish History and Literature*, edited by Isadore Twersky, 1: 82–109. Cambridge: Harvard University Press, 1979.

Pluralism Project, The. Harvard University. https://pluralism.org/.

Polyakov, Emma O'Donnell. *Antisemitism, Islamophobia, and Interreligious Hermeneutics: Ways of Seeing the Religious Other.* Leiden: Brill, 2019. https://doi.org/10.1163/9789004381674.

Porton, Gary. *Goyim: Gentiles and Israelites in Mishnah-Tosefta.* Providence: Brown Judaic Studies, 1988.

Pseudo-Dionysius. *Pseudo-Dionysius: The Complete Works.* Translated by Colm Luibheid. New York: Paulist Press, 1987.

Pugliese, Marc A. and Alexander Y. Hwang, eds. *Teaching Interreligious Encounters.* New York: Oxford University Press, 2017. https://doi.org/ 10.1093/oso/9780190677565.001.0001.

Putnam, Robert D., and David E. Campbell. *American Grace: How Religion Divides and Unites Us.* New York: Simon & Schuster, 2010.

Qadhi, Abu Amaar Yasir. *An Introduction to the Sciences of the Qur'an.* Birmingham: Al-Hidaayah, 1999.

Rabb, Intisar. *Doubt in Islamic Law: A History of Legal Maxims, Interpretation, and Islamic Criminal Law.* Cambridge: Cambridge University Press, 2017.

Ramelli, Ilaria L. E. *The Christian Doctrine of Apokatastasis.* Leiden: Brill, 2013. https://doi.org/10.1163/9789004245709.

Richardson, E. Allen. *Strangers in This Land: Religion, Pluralism, and the American Dream.* Jefferson: McFarland, 2010.

Rippin, Andrew. "Occasions of Revelation." In *Encyclopaedia of the Qur'ān*, edited by Jane Dammen McAuliffe, 569–573 Leiden: Brill, 2001–2006. https://doi.org/10.1163/1875-3922_q3_EQSIM_00305.

Rousseau, Jean-Jacques. *On the Social Contract, and the First and Second Discourses*. Edited and translated by Susan Dunn. New Haven: Yale University Press, 2002.

Rumi, Jalal al-Din Muhammad. *The Quatrains of Rumi*. Translated by Ibrahim Gamard and Rawan Farhadi. New York: Sufi Dari Books, 2008.

Saadia Gaon. *The Book of Beliefs and Opinions (Emunot veDeot)*. Translated by Samuel Rosenblatt. New Haven: Yale University Press, 1989.

Sachedina, Abdulaziz. *The Islamic Roots of Democratic Pluralism*. Oxford: Oxford University Press, 2001. https://doi.org/10.1093/acprof:oso/9780195 139914.001.0001.

"The Qur'ān and Other Religions." In *The Cambridge Companion to the Qur'ān*, edited by Jane Dammen McAuliffe, 291–309. Cambridge: Cambridge University Press, 2006. https://doi.org/10.1017/ CCOL0521831601.015.

Sacks, Jonathan. *The Dignity of Difference: How to Avoid the Clash of Civilizations*. London: Continuum, 2002.

Said, Edward W. *Orientalism*. New York: Vintage Books, 1979.

Schachter-Shalomi, Zalman M. "No Other." In *Broken Tablets: Restoring the Ten Commandments and Ourselves*, edited by Rachel S. Mikva, 21–24. Woodstock: Jewish Lights, 1999.

Schmidt-Leukel, Perry. *Religious Pluralism and Interreligious Theology*. Maryknoll: Orbis Books, 2017.

Sefaria: A Living Library of Torah Texts Online. www.sefaria.org.

Sahgal, Neha, Jonathan Evans, Ariana Monique Salazar, Kelsey Jo Starr, Manolo Corichi "Diversity and Pluralism." Pew Research Center. June 29, 2021. www.pewforum.org/2021/06/29/diversity-and-pluralism/.

Seligman, Adam B. *Living with Difference: How to Build Community in a Divided World*. Berkeley: University of California Press, 2015.

Shachter, Jack. *The Idea of Monotheism: The Evolution of a Foundational Concept*. Lanham: Hamilton Books, 2018.

Shafiq, Muhammad and Mohammed Abu-Nimer. *Interfaith Dialogue: A Guide for Muslims*. London: International Institute for Islamic Thought, 2011.

Shah-Kazemi, Reza. *The Spirit of Tolerance in Islam*. London: I. B. Tauris, 2012.

Shoemaker, Terry and James Edmonds. "The Limits of Interfaith? Interfaith Identities, Emerging Potentialities, and Exclusivity." *Culture and Religion*

17, no. 2 (May 2016): 200–212. https://doi.org/10.1080/14755610.2016 .1183688.

Siddiqui, Ataullah. *Christian–Muslim Dialogue in the Twentieth Century.* New York: St. Martin's Press, 1997.

Siddiqui, Mona. *Christians, Muslims, and Jesus.* New Haven: Yale University Press, 2013.

Sirry, Mun'im. "'Compete with One Another in Good Works': Exegesis of Qur'an Verse 5:48 and Contemporary Muslim Discourses on Religious Pluralism." *Islam and Christian–Muslim Relations* 20, no. 4 (2009): 424–438. https://doi.org/10.1080/09596410903194886.

Smith, Jonathan Z. *Relating Religion: Essays in the Study of Religion.* Chicago: University of Chicago Press, 2004.

Smith, Wilfred Cantwell. *The Meaning and End of Religion: A New Approach to the Religious Traditions of Mankind.* New York: Macmillan, 1962. https://doi.org/10.2307/j.ctv1hqdhgt.

Towards a World Theology: Faith and the Comparative History of Religion. Philadelphia: Westminster Press, 1981.

Soroush, Abdulkarim. *The Expansion of Prophetic Experience: Essays on Historicity, Contingency, and Plurality in Religion.* Translated by Nilou Mobasser. Leiden: Brill, 2009. https://doi.org/10.1163/ej.9789004171053. i-355.

Soukup, Charles and James Keaten. "Humanizing and Dehumanizing Responses across Four Orientations to Religious Otherness." In *A Communication Perspective on Interfaith Dialogue: Living Within the Abrahamic Traditions*, edited by Daniel S. Brown, Jr., 45–58. Lanham: Lexington Books, 2013.

Spivak, Gayatri Chakravorty. *Critique of Postcolonial Reason: Toward a History of the Vanishing Present.* Cambridge, MA: Harvard University Press, 1999. https://doi.org/10.2307/j.ctvjsf541.

Spitzer, Toba. "Why We Need Process Theology." *CCAR Journal: The Reform Jewish Quarterly* (Winter 2012): 84–95.

Stendahl, Krister. "From God's Perspective We Are All Minorities." *Journal of Religious Pluralism* 2 (1993). www.jcrelations.net/articles/article/from-gods-perspective-we-are-all-minorities.html.

Stopes-Roe, Harry. "Humanism as a Life Stance." *New Humanist* 103, no. 2 (October 1988): 19–21.

Suchocki, Marjorie Hewitt. *Divinity and Diversity: A Christian Affirmation of Religious Pluralism.* Nashville: Abingdon Press, 2003.

Swidler, Leonard, Khalid Duran, and Reuven Firestone. *Trialogue: Jews, Christians, and Muslims in Dialogue*. New London: Twenty-Third Publications, 2007.

Syeed, Najeeba and Heidi Hadsell, eds. *Critical Perspectives on Interreligious Education: Experiments in Empathy*. Leiden: Brill, 2020. https://doi.org/ 10.1163/9789004420045.

Townes, Emilie. *In a Blaze of Glory: Womanist Spirituality as Social Witness*. Nashville: Abingdon Press, 1995.

Upton, Charles. *The Way Forward for Perennialism: After the Antinomianism of Frithjof Schuon*. Hillsdale: Sophia Perennis, 2022.

Wadud, Amina. *Qur'an and Woman: Rereading the Sacred Text from a Woman's Perspective*. New York: Oxford University Press, 1999.

Wall, Robert. "Ecumenicity and Ecclesiology: The Promise of the Multiple Letter Canon of the New Testament." In *The New Testament as Canon*, edited by Robert Wall and Eugene Lemcio, 184–207. Sheffield: Sheffield Academic, 1992.

Wang, Robin R. "Yinyang." *Internet Encyclopedia of Philosophy*, https://iep .utm.edu/yinyang.

Wasserstrom, Steven. "Islamicate History of Religions?" *History of Religions* 27, no. 4 (1988): 405–411. https://doi.org/10.1086/463130.

Westermann, Claus. *Genesis 12–36: A Commentary*. London: SPCK, 1986.

White, Lauren Smelser. "For Comparative Theology's Christian Skeptics: An Invitation to Kenotic Generosity in the Religiously Pluralistic Situation." *Harvard Theological Review* 109, no. 2 (2016): 159–177. https://doi.org/ 10.1017/S0017816016000018.

Williams, Patrick and Laura Chrisman, eds. *Colonial Discourse and Post-Colonial Theory*. New York: Columbia University Press, 1994.

Williams, Rowan. "Christian Identity and Religious Plurality." Plenary Session address, World Council of Churches Assembly, Porto Alegre, 2006.

Wilson, Tom and Riaz Ravat. *Learning to Live Well Together: Case Studies in Interfaith Diversity*. London: Jessica Kingsley Publishers, 2017.

Winter, Tim. "The Last Trump Card: Islam and the Supersession of Other Faiths." *Studies in Interreligious Dialogue* 9, no. 2 (1992): 133–155. https://doi.org/10.2143/SID.9.2.2003988.

Wolf, Arnold Jacob. "The State of Jewish Belief." *Commentary* (August 1966). www.commentary.org/articles/jacob-agus–2/the-state-of-jewish-belief/.

Wuthnow, Robert. *America and the Challenges of Religious Diversity*. Princeton: Princeton University Press, 2005.

Acknowledgments

With deep gratitude for all the readers and dialogue partners—far too many to name. Thank you also to the wonderful staff at Cambridge University Press, who helped bring this project to fruition.

Cambridge Elements ≡

Religion and Monotheism

Paul K. Moser

Loyola University Chicago

Paul K. Moser is Professor of Philosophy at Loyola University Chicago. He is the author of *God in Moral Experience; Paul's Gospel of Divine Self-Sacrifice; The Divine Goodness of Jesus; Divine Guidance; Understanding Religious Experience; The God Relationship; The Elusive God* (winner of national book award from the Jesuit Honor Society); *The Evidence for God; The Severity of God; Knowledge and Evidence* (all Cambridge University Press); and *Philosophy after Objectivity* (Oxford University Press); coauthor of *Theory of Knowledge* (Oxford University Press); editor of *Jesus and Philosophy* (Cambridge University Press) and *The Oxford Handbook of Epistemology* (Oxford University Press); and coeditor of *The Wisdom of the Christian Faith* (Cambridge University Press). He is the coeditor with Chad Meister of the book series *Cambridge Studies in Religion, Philosophy, and Society.*

Chad Meister

Affiliate Scholar, Ansari Institute for Global Engagement with Religion, University of Notre Dame

Chad Meister is Affiliate Scholar at the Ansari Institute for Global Engagement with Religion at the University of Notre Dame. His authored and co-authored books include *Evil: A Guide for the Perplexed* (Bloomsbury Academic, 2nd edition); *Introducing Philosophy of Religion* (Routledge); *Introducing Christian Thought* (Routledge, 2nd edition); and *Contemporary Philosophical Theology* (Routledge). He has edited or co-edited the following: *The Oxford Handbook of Religious Diversity* (Oxford University Press); *Debating Christian Theism* (Oxford University Press); with Paul Moser, *The Cambridge Companion to the Problem of Evil* (Cambridge University Press); and with Charles Taliaferro, *The History of Evil* (Routledge, in six volumes). He is the co-editor with Paul Moser of the book series *Cambridge Studies in Religion, Philosophy, and Society.*

About the Series

This Cambridge Element series publishes original concise volumes on monotheism and its significance. Monotheism has occupied inquirers since the time of the Biblical patriarch, and it continues to attract interdisciplinary academic work today. Engaging, current, and concise, the Elements benefit teachers, researched, and advanced students in religious studies, Biblical studies, theology, philosophy of religion, and related fields.

Cambridge Elements ☰

Religion and Monotheism

Elements in the Series

A full series listing is available at: www.cambridge.org/er&m

Printed in the United States
by Baker & Taylor Publisher Services